SUNDAY ADELAJA

How to be
in the
HERE AND NOW

STOP DAYDREAMING
AND START LIVING

Sunday Adelaja

HOW TO BE IN THE HERE AND NOW

©2017 Sunday Adelaja

ISBN 978-1-908040-71-8

Copyright © Golden Pen Limited

Milton Keynes, United Kingdom. All rights reserved

WWW.GOLDENPENPUBLISHING.COM

Cover design by Oleksander Bondaruk

Interior design by Oleksander Bondaruk

© Sunday Adelaja, 2017,
How to be in the Here and Now — Milton Keynes, UK:
Golden Pen Limited, 2017

CONTENTS

INTRODUCTION

The Sleep of Reason Produces Monsters
SPANISH PROVERB

Have you ever heard people say, *"Life has passed like a dream"?* It is quite common to find people who have lived a considerable number of years but at the end of their life, they suddenly discover that their whole life was one of continuous sleep. The worst regret being that throughout their entire life, they did not bother to wake up.

One of the etchings by Francisco Goya (1746–1828), Spanish painter and engraver, one of the first and the most prominent artists of the Roman era, is called *"The Sleep of Reason"*. The artist accompanied it with the following explanation: *"When the mind sleeps, fantasy in sleepy dreams produces monsters, but in combination with the awakened mind, the fantasy becomes the mother of art and all his wonderful creations"*. Imagination combined with reason produces not monsters, but the wonderful works of art. But when we cease to control ourselves, cease to be IN THE HERE AND NOW, our minds are capable of creating such monsters that you can only be taken by surprise. But monsters are generated, not by the imagination itself, and not by reason, but precisely by the sleep of the latter. But the truth is that our MIND is DESIGNED to be VIGILANT. It is intended to restrain obsessive fantasies that possess the mind of man when he ceases to control himself, and every second, to realize himself in the HERE AND NOW.

What causes the daily events in our lives? For instance being asleep in reality whereby we are present in a particular place physically, yet our thoughts are soaring in the clouds, thinking about completely different things. How can we change the things we encounter every day? How can we reverse the verdict of fate we bring on ourselves by not living in the HERE AND NOW, the fate of sleeping through life and not waking up, leaving this world without really touching it? By not living this life HERE AND NOW, we waste it; we do not fully live. In fact, life passes by. Do you like this situation? Do you want to change this already established habit in your life that leads to nowhere? If 'yes', then do not hesitate to explore this book!

PRACTICAL ADVICE
FOR READING BOOKS

This book can change your life!

Often, when reading a book, we decide to apply every life lesson we gain. But much more often, after only a few weeks, we have completely forgotten about our intentions. You can have a lot of knowledge in your head but never apply it. Much of what you will read here will not be something new to you. The question is, what will you do with this knowledge?

Here are five practical ways that will at least allow you to turn your good intentions into good actions:

1. Read this book several times

Often stop reading the book to reflect on its content. Ask yourself, how and when you can apply a particular recommendation. After a detailed study of the book, re-read it every month, giving it a few hours. This book should become your 'desktop'.

2. Underline and make notes

While, reading this book, keep a highlighter pen. Emphasize individual lines of text and paragraphs — this simple action will triple your ability to remember. On the margins of the book, record your thoughts and make notes — let this book be your book. Underlining makes the book much more interesting and in the future helps to quickly identify the thoughts again.

3. Re-read the underlined parts

By underlining and annotation, you can quickly view the most important issues and parts of this book. To read the book and get the desired results, you have to review it as often as possible.

Let the selected parts inspire you to improve your life. As humans, we have an amazing ability to forget. The only way to retain the necessary information in memory is to return to it again and again.

4. Immediately apply the principles learned

Applying what is learned allows us to better understand and remember what is heard. It is impossible to teach a man anything; he can only learn. This means that learning is an active process. Most of all, we learn best through practice. If you want to master the principles outlined in this book, use them as often as possible and whenever possible. If you don't practice, you will soon forget. Only that which is applied can be retained in memory.

5. Give priority to what you learn

Select from one to three points, to start with. Start to constantly apply them until they become a habit. The practical benefits that you will derive from this book can become your habit only as a result of consistent application. Only in this way will you grow to use the knowledge unconsciously.

At the end of each Chapter you will find the Golden nuggets — a collection of all the important ideas expressed throughout the Chapter. You will also see tests to evaluate yourself and your skills, and practical exercises that will help you to translate what you've read into life. They are not just for reading. To help you get the maximum results and benefits from the practical tasks, we strongly recommend that you perform them within 24 hours, otherwise you will be overtaken by vanity; you will be once again distanced from your destiny, and those changes you expect in your life will never happen.

In my long experience with people, I know that usually people carry out similar assignments in a manner to "just make the grade". But you are not in school, where you get away with different levels of assignment responses. We are talking about your life. How much your life will change depends on the labour you put into building it. Therefore, I urge you to take the assignments seriously. These are not for the author of the book, but for you. To perform the tasks, it is desirable to find a quiet place where no one will be able to interfere with you. Perhaps it will be a time when no one is home, or the night when everyone is asleep, and nobody will disturb you.

Be sure to reflect on the previous Chapter, going over all the items you emphasized for yourself. Remember your decisions and write down your next steps. Don't forget to set a specific time frame as the restrictions that you will impose on yourself. This will help you not to postpone the planned steps towards changing your life by relegating them to the "back burner". Find someone to whom you could be accountable for your decisions, who could remind or partner with you to work on yourself.

Write down the date you start reading this book. Let that specific date be for you the beginning of a turning point in your life!

RECOMMENDATIONS ON CARRYING OUT THE PRACTICAL TASKS

1. ATTENTION! The practical tasks listed after each Chapter are not just for reading; you need them. With my years of experience with people, I know that oftentimes, people perform these tasks just 'to tick the box', as if in school; but this is your life, this is for you, take the assignments seriously.

2. For maximum results we recommend you perform the tasks within 24 hours, otherwise, leaving them for later, you are distancing yourself from your destiny and your success.

3. To answer all the questions, work out the practical tasks in a serene and tranquil environment. Find a quiet place where no one will be able to interfere; perhaps a time when no one is at home; or at night when everyone is asleep.

4. Be sure to reflect on the previous Chapter and go over all the items which you emphasized for yourself. Remember the decisions you made and write down your subsequent actions.

5. Certainly put specific time deadlines planned, and define restrictions which you will apply in relation to yourself; it will help you not to shelve implementation of the decisions you made.

6. Find someone to whom you could be accountable regarding your decisions, who could remind you of them — a kind of partner in working on yourself.

ADVICE
FOR PASSING THE TESTS

Tests listed after each chapter help you to analyze yourself and know your true position. After finding your weaknesses, you can strengthen them by using the principles given in this book. Answer the questions or approval tests honestly and thoughtfully. By so doing, you will help not only yourself, but other people in solving their problems as well.

You should mark only one answer in each question or approval test. The score is shown next to each answer in the parentheses. Your total score will indicate your readiness to become a 'personality' and not a 'biomass'. The tests help each person discover their true position or benchmark for change in their lives; and are not in any case intended to humiliate you. After all, for every one of us, there is always something to work on.

CHAPTER 1

A SCATTERBRAIN AND INATTENTIVENESS IS A MANIFESTATION OF A PERSON THAT IS NOT IN THE HERE AND NOW

"HERE IS A SCATTERBRAIN ON THE STREET POOL"

The clearest illustration of the fact that man does not live by the principle of the HERE AND NOW, is the poem by Samuil Yakovlevich Marshak, which was published in 1930. Before we turn to the solution of this problem, let's see how it manifests itself. If you recognize yourself in these sketches, be especially attentive to what you'll read next.

HERE IS A SCATTERBRAIN
Samuil Marshak

There was a scatterbrain
On the Street Pool.
He sat down on the bed in the morning,
He began to put on a jacket,

In the sleeves he slipped his hands —
It turned out, these were trousers.
Here is a scatterbrain
On the Street Pool!
He was putting on a coat —
They said to him, not that.
He began to pull the leggings —
They said to him, "That's not yours".
Here is a scatterbrain
On the Street Pool!
Instead of an outing cap
He put on a frying pan.
Instead of boots, gloves
Pulled himself on the heels.
Here is a scatterbrain
On the Street Pool!
Once on the tram
He went to the station
And opening the door,
He asked the agent, "Dear
At all costs
I want to go.
Is it possible to have a tram
Station stop?"
The agent was surprised:
The tram stopped.
Here is a scatterbrain
On the Street Pool!
He went to the snack bar
To buy himself a ticket.
And then rushed to the cashier
To buy a bottle of soda.
Here is a scatterbrain

On the Street Pool!
He ran to the platform,
Got into the train,
Brought his knots and suitcases,
He stuffed them under sofas,
He sat down in a corner before a window
And then He fell asleep into a quiet dream.
"What is this whistle-stop, for a sub-station?"
He shouted in a haze.
And from the platform speakers,
"This is the city of Leningrad."
He again had a little nap
And again he looked out the window,
Saw a large train station,
He was astonished and asked,
"What station is this?
Bologoye or Popovka?"
And from a platform speakers,
"This is the city of Leningrad."
Again he slept a little
And again, looked out the window,
Saw a large station,
Reached out and asked,
"What station is this?
Dibuna or Yamskaya?"
And from the platform speakers,
"It is the city of Leningrad."
He shouted, "What a joke!
I have travelled for two days,
And I am back,
Back to Leningrad!"
Here is a scatterbrain
On the Street Pool!

To be IN THE HERE AND NOW is a necessity! The consequence of not being so is that when it was time to dress up in the morning, all the clothes were mixed up; to put on a shirt he stretches himself into his trousers, instead of the cap — a pan, instead of the boots, gloves! And in addition, he lay claim to someone else's coat and leggings. A trip on public transport is also not without its oddities: his question to the agent can cause doubt concerning the sanity of the hero in this poem. The fact that he went to the snack bar to get the ticket, and to a ticket office for a bottle of soft drink, can bring a smile. Travelling on a train for two days can generally cause a hysterical laughter. The impression here is that people who are not living according to the principle of being IN THE HERE AND NOW can entertain others!

Such people often get trapped because of their carelessness. An example of a stunning story from Kiev is that of Valeria Zdanovskaya:

I had a ridiculous incident — After work, I went to the supermarket. I took the chicken, cheese, candy, a lot of different stuff. The whole basket was filled. I paid and left. Later on, I returned, of course, for the products, when I realized that I'd forgotten them. The staff happily greeted me. They'd since learned what I was. I did smile and played a finger to my temple. In my son's case, he manages to forget the school bag when going to school! My son regularly loses his cell phone, shoes, and sports pants. I have even lost the keys to the apartment. We have taken all acceptable measures! But still my son is regularly absent-minded! We almost accepted this. *"How could he be different, look at his mom!" says the father, sadly.*

"Well, it happens to everyone!" you would say. Is it really the lack of human presence? Is being IN THE HERE AND NOW the problem?

A WIDESPREAD BEHAVIOR OF COMMON PEOPLE

Alevtina came for a business meeting, which was appointed at the café in the city centre, being late for half an hour. Apologizing, this specialist psychologist with extensive private practice, leading business training, the mother of two adorable twins, suddenly complained that her life is "being wasted" right before her eyes and her "bad smell" is starting to haunt her everywhere. Today, for example, there was a very strange smell in her car, and the shop where she bought ice cream, and even on the Boulevard. Her companion sniffed, and realized that this is the truth: this really was not fragrant bread rolls and freshly brewed coffee, but she was carrying something frankly stale. Business negotiations continued for another five minutes, until Alevtina needed to get seminar brochures and plans for demonstration to her client. She dived into her package, carefully located under the table, and looked out from there all red from embarrassment. The smell that has just been maintaining a presence, became unbearable. It turned out that Alevtina has been mistakenly carrying around everywhere a garbage bag that, in the morning, was meant to go into the bin. Most likely, she left the package of materials in the hallway at the front door. The good thing with this story was that the doc-

uments were not disposed of as garbage; they were just forgotten at home.

How many of these stories could each one of us remember? In our daily lives, almost every one of us suffers from inattentiveness and distraction. Quite often we forget to make important calls to congratulate people close to us with a birthday or other important dates; we forget to fulfill a promise; to keep our word, to buy all the necessary products. We forget to pick a child up from kindergarten or to charge our mobile phone in time. We spend a long time in school or at work, leaving late or missing an important meeting; we lose keys, wallets, umbrellas, cell phones, get involved in accidents, the list goes on.

We lose a thought in mid-sentence or forget what we had just read or heard. We are easily distracted from present tasks, chronically short of time; we undercook food whenever we try to prepare a dish, we forget to water the house plants and so they wither. We can pour boiling water into the sugar bowl instead of the teapot, or not arrive at the right airport for our vacation journey just because we did not bother to carefully study the information on the ticket. It is said that once a terrorist pushes their demands on the telephone, he has just introduced his real name.

The reason for all that has been described above is that they are **the actions we perform through inertia or mechanically, in other words not being HERE AND NOW.** This confusion is often caused not by the poor memory of man nor the lack of attention to some of the everyday things that are so needed at a particular time. Most of the unpleasant cases with forgetfulness are associated with automatic actions. For example, we unconsciously lock the car door, and then cannot remember, was it locked or not. Or we add salt to the soup while talking to a neighbor at a table, and then after a few minutes, we reach for the salt shaker again.

Distraction or inattentiveness can manifest through the inability to focus and finish a task. This is mainly due to the fact that a person's attention is superficial; and so it easily switches to a secondary task in the middle of performing the first one — the person is easily distracted. Another example of such a manifestation is starting to read the morning newspapers and then being distracted by the need to check the emails. Before he has time to reply to the e-mails, this person's attention shifts to the work-place site; he needs to check the schedule for the day (on that very day)! As a result, concentration levels drop, productivity and efficiency declines and scheduled tasks remain unfinished.

A striking example of the behavior of such a person is Khlestakov from *"The Inspector"* by Gogol, who was unable to focus his attention on one thought. In every single moment, his attention was directed towards whatever subject appears before his eyes, whatever randomly occurred to him at that moment. Here's how the writer describes the character, *"He is unable to stop the constant attention on any thought"*. His attention could easily jump from one subject to another. There is an inability to concentrate on and to perform anything, because of superficial attention and very high distractions. Here you can note the lack of a conscious effort to focus on a particular task until it is done. Such inattentiveness is typical and natural for a child due to the immaturity of the nervous system. For adults, similar distractions become the source of many of life's problems.

Here are a couple of examples:

- A student unable to concentrate asked for help:
  "Hello, I am doing R&D work for a reputed firm. I am also doing my Ph.D. from the same field. My problem is that I am not able to concentrate while reading or studying. And my work requires a lot of reading. So my productivity has become very low. If I spent a whole day studying, I would have read a couple of pages!! When I start to work a lot of thoughts distract me. I feel like eating, surfing the Web, if at home to watch TV etc. So my performance is being affected. This problem appeared about 2 years ago. Until that I was a very studious girl, and was always a topper in my life. I tried things like meditation, but it does not seem to work. Please help me."

- One woman complained about her husband,
  "My husband is very absent-minded. It has gotten to a stage where there are labels everywhere; on the fridge — 'Close the fridge', over the ironing board — 'Switch off the iron', the list goes on. Most evenings, we search for flash drives while in the mornings, keys, wallet and phone. These searches often lead to nothing. What do I do? Help!»

People who suffer from such negligence usually have difficulties being organised in both their work and personal life. They need to make some effort to fit into a common framework.

Lack of being IN THE HERE AND NOW can manifest in the following:

- A superficial glance on events;
- Defocused attention;
- Easily distracted by extraneous things;
- Forgetfulness.

Most people live half here and half somewhere else, as if they are sleeping in reality, mentally absent, although physically present. Such people live 'on autopilot', 'fly away thoughts', 'hang', or 'fall' from reality. If you try to call back such a person to reality, he justifies himself that he was 're-flecting'. If you ask him to repeat what was said before, the man finds it difficult to do. This phenomenon is captured by the expression — *"daydreaming"*. That means *"forming a pleasant visionary, usually wishful mental, image of something that is not present or that is not the case, and unlikely to be fulfilled, during wakefulness"*.

The daydreamer is:

- One who indulges in useless and absent-minded thoughts and dreams,
- A person that avoids reality and lives in a world of illusions, fantasies, and finally
- A person who does not perform well in their tasks, they are usually lazy or a mediocre.

Unlike the usual dreams, daydreams and fantasies relate to things that are unrealizable, unreal; but a dream is what we are going to put into life. For example, you may dream to go to the Canary Islands or write a book. But when you imagine that you are like a bird flying in the clouds or that you are the president of Japan, these are fantasies! It is usually difficult to interact with such people. In what reality do these people live? In which clouds are they soaring?

An example of a fancy **way of thinking or inclination** to 'soaring in the clouds' is the heroine of Gogol — Ivan Fedorovich Shponki, *"Vasilisa Kashparovna wanted to marry Shponka and dreamt of grandchildren."* Here's how the behavior of this type of people was described by the great Russian novelist, playwright, poet, critic, essayist, recognized as one of the classics of Russian literature, Nikolai Gogol (1809–1852): *"Often, making some pastries, which she generally never trusted with the cook, she, imagining that near her stands a little grandson asking for a pie, absent-mindedly holds out a hand to him with the best piece. The yard dog, using this, grips the tasty morsel and by its loud chomping sound would lead her out of her daydream, and was always a bit of a poker."* This means that someone can be so absorbed in their fantasies and dreams that they completely 'drop out' from reality. The problem is that it does not go unnoticed.

ABSENT-MINDEDNESS IS NOT AS HARMLESS AS IT MAY SEEM AT FIRST SIGHT

In Slavic mentality, including the modern era created partly during the Soviet period, Absent-mindedness and non-concentration was never a terrible sin. It is considered that Absent-mindedness is along the line of personality peculiarity, as a rule, to kind and honest people. Each of us, probably, remembers the remarkable movie of Leonid Gaidai 'A Diamond Arm', one of the most popular films in the history of the Soviet cinema. The main character is a hapless Semen Semenovich Gorbunkov (actor Yuri Nikulin), cooperating with the police, conspires to use a taxi, the driver of which is the policeman.

Once Gorbunkov was given a wad of money and a gun 'just in case', Gorbunkov takes the money and gun and puts them in his shopping bag, where he previously put the bread, and was going to get out of the car. The startled police officer, disguised as a taxi driver, who gave Gorbunkov weapons and money, says reproachfully:

"Semen Semenych! Are you well?"

In this case, Semen Semenovich grabs his head and puts the gun in his pocket:
"Ah-ah-ah!"

This scene from the movie is unforgettable, and the phrase 'Semen Semenych!' was the catch. It made this episode the epitome of a cute Soviet man, the only drawback being inattentiveness.

Often in our society the absence of the person in the HERE AND NOW tends to be considered as a sign of a genius. Who does not remember the hero of Jules Verne's book *'The Children of Captain Grant'* - Professor Paganel, an extremely absent-minded scientist? This Geographer got on the ship and instead of sailing to India, went to South America — Chile. He had taken a nap to avoid sea-sickness and found out about the mistake after 35 hours of peacefully sleeping! For the needs of the expedition, he started learning the Spanish language in the poem 'Louisiana', only to later discover that the author of the poem was a Portuguese and the work is written in Portuguese, not Spanish. Wounded Lord Glenarvan wrote the order to be transferred with the yacht 'Duncan', but absent-mindedly wrote 'New Zealand', instead of 'Australia', thereby sending the 'Duncan' a couple of hundred kilometers to the North. The only positive thing from the Absent-mindedness of the scientist is that the error of Paganel ultimately saved the lives of the members of the expedition, confusing the maps and destroying the evil plans of Ayrton — Ben Joyce. This is a cute literary character about the adventures which we know from childhood. The wrong thing in it is how this romantic and altruist Jacques Paganel behaves.

Although this Absent-mindedness and carelessness is amusing and seems harmless at first sight, a person who doesn't live every minute in the HERE AND NOW poses serious threat to the safety of others. The gas which isn't turned off due to Absent-mindedness, the iron that is not switched off, driving the car on "autopilot", crossing the street while staring at the clouds or the distracted air traffic controller — all these can lead to tragedy.

In the society, the spread of the phenomenon of not being IN THE HERE AND NOW is economically disadvantageous. *"Researchers conclude that people suffering from absent-mindedness, perform just at the '11-month' rate. In other words, they spend a month on something that distracts them"*, writes Forbes. A Consulting firm, Basex estimates that such distractions like phone calls and non-business emails, take away from Americans 28% of working time a day. If we calculate the economic damage, it will be 650 billion dollars a year. Just think about it for a moment! Every year, 650 billion dollars is lost due to negligence!

Probably at any other time, you would continue to live and work with that quality level. However today, when the time poses new challenges, when the speed and accuracy of actions depends on the success of almost all our deeds and undertakings, distraction and lack of focus can seriously harm everyone. The present time dictates that qualities like discipline, punctuality and ability to be IN THE HERE AND NOW every second, are necessary in making one responsible and able to penetrate deep into any matter, without superficiality, and carefully understand it. Absent-mindedness is neither desirable nor funny, it is a very serious problem that makes friends, family and colleagues to never take you seriously.

To defeat absent mindedness and inattentiveness, we must learn to live in the HERE AND NOW, and not be carried away by thoughts into unknown worlds. It is time to stop sticking your head in the clouds and indulging in unrealistic fantasies and dreams. Not being IN THE HERE AND NOW may be quite acceptable for some, but it obviously doesn't fit in with today's realities, which pose new challenges to the discipline and responsibility of a person. In the next Chapter we will give more consideration to what happens when people do not live according to the principle of HERE AND NOW.

GOLDEN NUGGETS

1. The reason for Absent-mindedness and inattentiveness is often due to the fact that we accomplish our actions by inertia, it is mechanical.

2. Inattentiveness manifests itself in:
   a. A cursory glance at what is happening;
   b. Defocused attention;
   c. Easily distracted by extraneous things;
   d. Forgetfulness.

3. Absent-mindedness and inattentiveness are the result of a lack of ability to concentrate

4. People can so indulge in their fantasies and dreams to the extent that they completely "escape" from reality

5. Lack of being IN THE HERE AND NOW can lead to tragedy

6. Inattention costs about 650 billion dollars a year

7. Absent-mindedness and inattentiveness are not desirable human traits, but are terrible symptoms that you need to pay attention to

8. Organization and punctuality plus the ability to be IN THE HERE AND NOW every second, are necessary qualities of an adult whose behavior is characterized by responsibility and ability to penetrate deep into any matter, without superficiality, and carefully understand it.

SELF ASSESSMENT

1. When playing any game, how often do you lose because of carelessness?

   a) Very often (0)
   b) Sometimes (1)
   c) Rarely (3)
   d) Never (4)

2. Can you simultaneously work and listen to what they say around you?

   a) This is unreal! (0)
   b) No (1)
   c) With some difficulty (2)
   d) Yes (4)

3. Do you carefully look both sides before you cross the street?

   a) No (0)
   b) Rarely (1)
   c) Mostly, Yes (3)
   d) Always (4)

4. Are you offended when you are interrupted or disturbed in the middle of carrying out a task?

   1. Often (0)
   2. Sometimes (1)
   3. Rarely (3)
   4. Never (4)

5. Do you always check your loose change?

   a) No (0)
   b) Rarely (1)
   c) Very often (3)
   d) Always (4)

ASSESSMENT TEST RESULTS

0–5 points

I'm sorry, but you're so dreamy and very scattered. And while many adversities pass just because you did not notice, but still need to be more careful to avoid unpleasant surprises. Reading this book and carrying out all the practical tasks will help remedy the situation. Enjoy your further reading!

6–10 points

You are quite scattered and love to dream, fortunately, in moderation. Further reading of this book and carrying out all practical tasks will help you become more alert and get rid of absent mindedness.

11–14 points

Excited for you! You care enough to manage your affairs and not forget anything important. Continued reading of this book and carrying out the exercises at the end of each Chapter will help you to strengthen your ability to be IN THE HERE AND NOW.

15–20 points

Congratulations! You are extremely vigilant and meticulous, nothing will deceive or hold you back. Such a memory and attention can only be envied! Be one of those that share the correct views on this life with others!

RECOMMENDATIONS ON CARRYING OUT THE PRACTICAL TASKS

1. ATTENTION! The practical tasks listed after each Chapter are not just for reading; you need them. With my years of experience with people, I know that oftentimes, people perform these tasks just 'to tick the box', as if in school; but this is your life, this is for you, take the assignments seriously.

2. For maximum results we recommend you perform the tasks within 24 hours, otherwise, leaving them for later, you are distancing yourself from your destiny and your success.

3. To answer all the questions, work out the practical tasks in a serene and tranquil environment. Find a quiet place where no one will be able to interfere; perhaps a time when no one is at home; or at night when everyone is asleep.

4. Be sure to reflect on the previous Chapter and go over all the items which you emphasized for yourself. Remember the decisions you made and write down your subsequent actions.

5. Certainly put specific time deadlines planned, and define restrictions which you will apply in relation to yourself; it will help you not to shelve implementation of the decisions you made.

6. Find someone to whom you could be accountable regarding your decisions, who could remind you of them — a kind of partner in working on yourself.

PRACTICAL TASKS

1. Recall and write down five examples from your life when you showed forgetfulness and absent mindedness. Investigate what was the cause of this behavior.

2. Analyze what ideas of Absent-mindedness and inattentiveness you have absorbed since childhood due to your environment (family, school, relatives, classmates, public opinion and so on). Identify what perceptions were wrong and what you need to fix or change in your thinking.

3. Are you a dreamer or visionary? How real are the dreams that you cherish in your heart? Do you have plans for practical implementation of your dreams? What exactly are you already doing at the moment to turn your dreams into reality?

CHAPTER 2

WHAT HAPPENS WHEN PEOPLE DO NOT LIVE ACCORDING TO THE PRINCIPLE OF BEING IN THE HERE AND NOW

In the previous Chapter we looked at the manifestations of the absence of being IN THE HERE AND NOW as Absent-mindedness and inattentiveness. In this Chapter, I want to suggest that you consider the following consequences when people do not live according to the principle of being HERE AND NOW.

Vasilisa lived in one of the finest places near Kiev with her husband and son (a second grader). Every day, after the husband leaves for work and her son to school, she goes to the city. In her car while coming from her son's school, Vasilisa would put herself in absent-minded mode. One day when she was returning home, she thought it was strangely quiet in the car. Turning around, Vasilisa was horrified — her son was not there! She pulled back. The bewildered child still stood rooted to the spot on the sidewalk, from where Vasilisa's car drove off about fifteen minutes ago. When the boy finally got into the car, confused, he told his mother, "You looked at me and left...".

Vasilisa was sure that the child got in the car and even remembers closing the door of the car behind him. At first she, of course, was very worried that she is a "bad mother". And then she read the news that went around all the tabloids of the world, and this partly reassured her. It turns out that Vasilisa was not the only one who suffers from memory lapses, taking her child from school. The wife of British Prime Minister Cameron had also experienced a similar situation. She went to the pub with her husband and took along their three children: her son who was six years old and two daughters — eight and two. The family had dinner. The older girl went to the toilet while the rest went to their cars; first — the father (Prime Minister), the second — mother with her son and the younger daughter, and they left. And the family forgot about the eldest daughter! Neither dad nor mom remembered her! It was until they got home that the parents discovered someone is missing and only then did they go back for their daughter.

I wonder in what kind of reality these people live? You know, while in school back then in my home village that had only forty houses, we were made to understand that one had to be IN THE HERE AND NOW, every minute and every second of one's life, rather than flying away in one's thoughts to some unknown fantasies. In this small village, school was a routine; if the teacher caught a student on such thought fantasies while in the classroom, he 'opened' the student's eyes. There was no conscious perception of this issue. The teacher used a smack as 'educational tool' and explained to the student the need to be IN THE HERE AND

NOW. A real war was declared then, on the repercussion of this phenomenon that we are trying to explore in this book.

The consequences of such behaviour, not to be IN THE HERE AND NOW, were clearly demonstrated to the students. This forced me to be conscious of this problem from as early as thirteen years of age, but unfortunately today, very few adults are aware of this and pay little attention to it, not to mention children and teenagers. Few people attach importance to being IN THE HERE AND NOW when they are listening, watching or talking. It doesn't come to mind that the absence of a man from being IN THE HERE AND NOW carries some danger, and may have serious consequences to our mental and intellectual health. Judging by how this phenomenon is prevalent in our world, we rarely pay enough attention to it while raising our children. On the contrary, the world system is built in such a way that even one does not want to 'disconnect' and fly away in their thoughts, they are not helped to do so.

To see how the Communist system was built and its consequences on the people in their way of thinking, attitudes and behavior, we recommend that you carefully study the work of George Orwell's 'Animal Farm'. Then you will see that in the former Soviet Union, for any man to feel confident, strong and famous, it was necessary to 'switch off' with the aid of alcohol. In those days, the entire population was drinking, otherwise it was impossible to survive. A sober man could not get acquainted with a woman, nor communicate and celebrate with friends. Even married women could not sleep with their husbands being sober. The reason for this phenomena is that the system tried to turn a man into an animal, so he would not think seriously about anything, but be convinced that 'the party will think for him'. Having a 'disconnected' mind made life easier, the voice of conscience was not a burden. In such a state, it was easier to be shameless, immoral and act like an animal!

WHAT IS THE DIFFERENCE BETWEEN MAN AND ANIMAL

If happiness lay in bodily pleasures, we would call oxen happy when they find vetch to eat.

HERACLITUS

You should know that when a person is 'sedated', when he is not HERE AND NOW, he ceases to be a reasoning man (Homo sapiens), because at that time he is not in use of his mind. Remember it's only at the moment when a person reasons with his mind, when he is HERE AND NOW, that he is actually a 'man'. **But whenever a person does not function through his reasoning, but just obeying instincts, then he is as good as an 'animal'.**

Instinct is an innate ability of living organisms to, quite unconsciously, response to a change in the internal or external environment with a corresponding action. Examples of such changes include: danger, hunger, fatigue and need for sleep, the necessity of procreation, etc. Instincts are the basis of the behavior of animals and children up to 5–7 years. Each of you can easily imagine the lifestyle of any street dog that wakes up in the nearest trash to find something to fill its stomach, no matter the quality of the food, sees a specimen of the opposite sex, runs to satisfy its instincts for reproduction. While the sun is shining it lies on the street — no worries, no hassles. In the evening, it huddles in some basement to sleep, and life goes on like this day by day. This is the meaningless animal life, not subordinated to any reasoning nor values, but just based on instincts and reflexes.

It turns out that there are people who live almost in the same scenario; living, avoiding stress, as if disconnected from reality, carried by life currents, doing everything automatically. Such people wake up in the morning not because they have a purpose for which they live, but because they know that a person has to wake up in the morning like all other people. They go to work in the same unconscious state, "We need to go somewhere, just like everybody else". So each morning this person gets up and carries his poor and miserable self to go to the job he hates. Every day is the same — at work in the morning and in the evening he's at home — dinner, TV, sleep and in the morning, he starts all over again. While young, they lose time and have fun with friends. As soon as the number of unmarried friends and girlfriends is reduced and all have pushchairs with children, they, without understanding the purpose of marriage, they immediately look for a mate, marry and have children. This is very similar to the animal life. And it is sad that this is the life that the majority of those living on the earth have chosen for themselves.

Obeying instincts and not guided by logic, makes people to react to events instead of initiating them. Their choices, determined by external circumstances and actions, are in response to external stimulation. As in Pavlov's experiments on dogs, the saliva and gastric juice was associated with the turning on of light bulbs. Thus, if there is a stimulus — light, that is, the response is the secretion of saliva and gastric juice by the animal. The man who does not live by reasoning, reacts to situations just like these dogs. You only have to touch or step on the pet, and it immediately reacts emotionally, instead of logically weighing, reflecting and reasoning to decide how to respond or whether to prudently take no notice and remain silent.

Many of us are basically just reacting to life. We do not create our life: we go to school because everybody does so, take on a profession because it is popular, without asking questions like: "What am I going to do?" "Why am I here at all?" "Where am I going?" "What is the mission of my life?" We get married because our friends got married, following the traditions and existing well-established notions in the society. Then when children are born, we don't even know what to do with them, how to bring them up.

Many people want to take credit for exactly how many children they have had through reproduction. In the former Soviet Union, mothers with many children were even given an award with a rank 'Mother Heroine', as the highest distinction for their merits in the birth and upbringing of children. But we must remember that this title was established in the years of the Great Patriotic War that took millions of lives, when the population dropped significantly. The State system then tried to use such measures to make up for the decline in the population and this gave rise to numerous generations of builders of communism. In the past, Africa's mortality rate was very high due to lack of medical facilities and families needed to preserve their lineage and therefore had many children. But do we still live for these purposes?

It may sound good to be the mother of five children or the father of ten but what distinguishes us as human beings from animals, is not the number of offspring. Any dog or cat, which at one time may give birth to a litter of ten or more, can win any competition. In order to have offspring, not a lot of reasoning is necessary, in fact, it does not need ANY reasoning — only instincts. People with an intellectual disability, speech problems are able to have children, their disability does not prevent them from having children. So becoming the father or mother of any number of children is not a reason for pride. But public opinion, our mothers and grandmothers, keep telling our daughters and grandchildren, "You're still not married?" "You haven't given birth yet?" The impression is that what makes a woman a 'human being' is whether she is married or not. Therefore, procreation is not what distinguishes man from animal. THE ONLY THING THAT DISTINGUISHES HUMANS FROM ANIMALS IS THAT MAN CAN ACT CONSCIOUSLY.

WHAT DOES IT MEAN TO LIVE CONSCIOUSLY

Consciousness is when a person is HERE AND NOW. Only during this period of time is the man a reasoning creature. The rest of the time he lives like an animal. To act consciously is the greatest opportunity, the greatest privilege God has given us. Only when we act consciously are we 'Homo sapiens'. Consciousness is what distinguishes people from animals and allows them to understand their own actions, to know their inner world and at the same time, understand the external world.

Just as the thermometer indicates whether it is cold or hot, our minds show the different levels of our sleep and wakefulness. Most of us know that there are different levels of sleep, but few people know that there are also varying degrees of wakefulness. And the degree of wakefulness depends on how alert the person is — that is, being IN THE HERE AND NOW- in their daily lives. The higher the level of wakefulness, the more accurate the vision of reality. Awakening is not always associated with that moment when we biologically wake up. Even when we are biologically awake, we can continue to 'sleep' through life. Moreover, we can live a lifetime without awakening.

We are not created to live by instincts or reflexes. We are created by God as Homo sapiens — which means that EVERY STEP SHOULD BE DONE CONSCIOUSLY. The man that is living every second of his life in the HERE AND NOW, that is, living consciously, acts in the everyday life in the following way: by reasoning he is able to choose from the available food, that which is more suited for his proper nutrition — if it requires him to wait for a while for the food to be ready, then that person is willing to wait. On the other hand, the man, who like an animal is driven by instincts, rises in the morning, indiscriminately eats any and everything, everything that catches his eye. In the end, the one who lives consciously is more healthy, has more energy and is in better physical shape than anyone else. Thus, the reasoning man prolongs his life to the time allocated for him, to as much as possible, reveal all the gifts and talents in fulfilling his calling and to achieve the purpose for which he came to the earth.

The man who is always HERE AND NOW, does not react to outside influence but rather chooses his own reactions to what is happening around. Moreover, the reasoning man initiates his actions, ahead of any impact on himself and forms the desired response. Such a person is proactive in the sense that he is fully aware of his values and goals, acting in accordance with his vital principles; and not on the dictates of conditions and circumstances. By acting consciously, he creates his own conditions and circumstances. ALL THAT MAN DOES UNCONSCIOUSLY — OBEYING INSTINCTS AND LIVING IN A DAYDREAM, HE DOES SO BY FOLLOWING THE CROWD, LIKE A 'GREY MASS'.

IF A PERSON DOES NOT LIVE ACCORDING TO THE PRINCIPLE OF BEING IN THE HERE AND NOW, HE BECOMES A GREY MASS

Ninety-five percent of people who walk the earth are simply inert.
Stephen King

Many people living in the modern world do not feel the need to think, to be IN THE HERE AND NOW. Many of us live 'mechanically', like a vending machine. Women mostly prefer to feel and experience while men would like to pursue and achieve. On the one hand, the 'automation' makes life easy but on the other hand, it deprives us of the opportunity to see, experience and enjoy every moment of this life — to notice the beauty of life around us. Because almost everything is done automatically, we are actually asleep in reality; and at this time we do not notice that life goes on following its course, and is passing us by. And then the person waiting for life, every day, lives aimlessly. This is the way of life for most ordinary people — a life without consciousness.

What are the characteristics of the 'grey mass', to which the person who isn't living by the principle of HERE AND NOW belongs? 'Grey mass' is a term that we associate with the faceless crowd of people who have no world view and therefore are always ready to submit. **A person gets used to living that way. He knows no other life, and doesn't even try to break out of this vicious circle to learn what lies beyond its limits.** Such a person is 'spiritually dead', but he seems to be normal — walking about, looking, talking and eating. He buys a sausage and without 'waking up', eats it. After a while, he goes out again to buy another sausage. This person physically lives on for 50, 60, 70 years. And when the time comes for him to die, he says to himself, "I should die..." and then leaves this world. But did this person die on the day of his physical death? Actually such a person died much earlier! A MAN FUNCTIONING WITHOUT REGAINING CONSCIOUSNESS, SLEEP-WALKING THROUGH LIFE, DAYDREAMING IN REALITY, NOT LIVING IN THE HERE AND NOW, THIS MAN DIED DURING HIS PHYSICAL LIFE. We die when we skip life — every moment of its existence.

In this regard, Benjamin Franklin made a remarkable statement, "Many people die at the age of 25, and get to the grave only at 75". This is precisely because they live and go through life on 'autopilot', sleep-walking. But life is not intended for that kind of existence, it is not intended for the human mind to be in a sleeping state. The 'sleep of reason' produces not only monsters, as we read with you in the introduction to this book. The 'sleep of reason' leads to death — premature death; when the person seems to be alive physically, but dead in his spirit, his mind, his soul. Life means LIVING WITH A PURPOSE, the purpose for which a person is born on this earth. Discover your calling and fulfil it. As soon as we stop pursuing that goal, life becomes a mere existence — and man ceases to be a human being. He becomes, in essence, a walking corpse. That is why it is so important to live in the HERE AND NOW.

Vladimir Lobanov described this type of life in a poem: *Grey Mass Lifestyle*. Look how well the poet managed to convey the attitude and the basic content of the lives of these people in only a hundred words:

LIFE IN 100 WORDS
Vladimir Lobanov

Cradle. Diapers. Crying.

Word. Step. Colds. Doctor.

Bustle. Toys. Brother.

Yard. Swing. Kindergarten.

School. "Two". "Three". "Five".

Ball. Tripping. Plaster. Bed.

Fight. Blood. Broken nose.

Courtyard. Friends. Party. Swagger.

Institute. Spring. Bushes.

Summer. Session. Tails.

Beer. Vodka. Gin with ice.

Coffee. Session. Diploma.

Romanticism. Love. Star.

Hands. Lips. Night without sleep.

Wedding. Mother-in-law. Father-in-law. Trap.

Quarrel. Club. Friends. Glass.

House. Work. House. Family.

Sun. Summer. Snow. Winter

Son. Diapers. Cradle.

Stress. Mistress. Bed.

Business. Money. Plan. All hands on deck.

Tv Set. TV. Series.

Giving. Cherries. Vegetable marrows.

Grey hair. Migraine. Glasses.

Grandson. Diapers. Cradle.

Stress. Pressure. Bed.

Heart. Kidneys. Bones. Doctor.

Speeches. Coffin. Good-bye. Crying.

These people — the 'grey mass', very often are referred to as rednecks or unicellular. Their entire life consists of: being born, growing up and going to school, then work, marriage, retirement and lastly, death. Their desire is too mundane and petty, their goal is too material, their interests and joy — primitive. It is the greyish mass that puts dictators in power, from their consent, concentration camps were built, including weapons of mass destruction.

The main characteristic of the grey mass category of people is that they are conformists. Such a person was described by the eminent Russian psychiatrist, P. B Ganushkin, in the early twentieth century. Gannushkin identified the following main characteristics of this people group:

1. Inability to think differently from the majority, especially to rise against the opinion of the majority.

2. Stereotyped thinking

3. A commitment to life morals and uttering statements with the cleverest platitudes.

4. Conservative in their political and economic views

5. Distrust of everything new

6. Difficulty in meeting new people

7. Lack of initiative

"BAD HEAD DOESN'T GIVE REST TO THE FEET"

Folk wisdom, as always, hits the nail on the head saying, *"a bad (i.e. useless) head gives no rest to the feet"* — talking of **one who doesn't think through their actions in advance — jerking off, anxious, fussing in vain, busy with too many things, running around.** This refers to a silly and confused person. Apparently, in our time, it isn't necessary to think at all; you can do as others say and do pretty well. You can live by your feelings — without reasoning, and in most cases, this will be enough.

To engage the mind in thinking is not just acting like a machine — automatically following worked out rules, being guided by previously obtained solutions and algorithms of habitual actions. To have a head on your shoulders is to have a reasoning mind — the ability to:

1. Engage your **mind in the active mode,** when attention is focused and concentrated
2. Act **consciously**
3. Orchestrate all events to lead to **the achievement of a desired goal**
4. Consider the **implications** and **conclusions**

To think means to include one's reasoning and attention to actively and independently engage in solving arising problems. Sometimes I am shocked by my assistants, because their actions are a bright illustrations of the saying given above: "THE BAD HEAD DOES NOT GIVE REST TO THE FEET!" Often in their engagements, as soon as they obtain a task, they grab it with both hands and feet and rush to execute the instructions, ignoring the first phase in the task implementation: the stage of analysis and design of an optimal algorithm for implementing the task. Sometimes I get the impression that we often completely forget why we are have a 'head'. It seems that for many people, the head is a kind of decoration designed only to beautify one's appearance — the head is great for displaying different hairstyles and the face — a facade of the head so to speak, can be decorated with stunning makeup!

I have the impression that few people remember the fact that the head is the brain and its main function is to think! And the question that I used to ask every now and then was, "Why not think before you act?" I now understand that this is not always applicable, because it's so much easier for us to live without thinking — not engaging our brain in its intended purpose.

Friends, I want to say to you that in this life, you have to think! Whatever you've got to do, you cannot take another step to the right hand nor to the left without first examining it, without reflection. The most important training of every human life is to THINK, to PONDER. Aimless or useless chatter and actions serving no pre-determined purpose are a sign that the person does not think. On the other hand, asking accurate and deep questions, qualitative analysis and making appropriate conclusions are a sign that the person thinks.

A typical example of the grey mass, who never troubles his head to think at all and as a result, keeps his legs constantly busy, is well described in the poem by Oksana Stork. Even the name speaks for itself — the life of such a person turns into a race, rushing '*without feeling sorry for the feet*', such that there is no time to even think.

PEOPLE RUN THROUGH LIFE, NOT SPARING THE LEGS
Oksana Aistov

People run through life, not sparing the legs:
Home — work, home — work, while serving time.
Weekend holidays as a respite.
The old age pension, shortness of breath, did you flee here?
Maybe you originally chose the wrong route?
Rise at seven in the morning, is the brain alive?
Someone sees the sun, the stars, why not you?
Management, production — not to beauty.
No time to breathe, a struggle every day.
For a corner crust of pension. You say, "Destiny."
Maybe, if you humbly accept it.
Soul, filled with sleeping pills to fall into oblivion,
In a series of soapsuds look for a rainbow,
Believe in the nursing home, and calmly wait.
Wait, till your children's legs get stronger,
The beaten track, they flee now.
Were you born for this purpose? And for this you lived?
Was it for happiness that you waited, dreamed, studied, loved and believed in?
If not, then, perhaps, slow down the pace. And start all over again — a new man.

Such is our life. So are people who live in the 'sedated' state, operating unconsciously, in obedience to the demands of their instincts. But it is important for us to understand, dear reader, that this is profitable to a system that wants to make each of us a 'little screw' that serves its interests. That's why we should stop sleep-waking and living at the animal level. We urgently need to wake up and get back on our feet! It's time to become a great person, and not an appendage to the system of this world! And for this we need to learn to live in the HERE AND NOW every second of our existence. Otherwise our psychiatric hospitals will continue to increase in number, but we'll discuss this in the next Chapter.

GOLDEN NUGGETS

1. When a person is 'sedated', when he is not HERE AND NOW, then he ceases to be a reasoning human being.

2. Only at the moment when a person engages his brain, when he is HERE AND NOW, that he is a man.

3. Whenever a man does not 'use his head' as he lives, just obeying instincts, he's as good as an animal.

4. In order to have offspring, a lot of mental activity is not necessary.

5. The only thing that distinguishes humans from animals is that man can act consciously.

6. The higher the level of wakefulness, the more accurate the vision of reality.

7. We must take every step consciously.

8. All that man does in obedience to the instincts, he does so while living in a dream and unconscious, he is following the crowd, like a grey mass.

9. If you live, without regaining consciousness, sleeping on the go in reality, if you do not live HERE AND NOW, your death occurs during your physical life.

SELF-ASSESSMENT

1. **Can you insist on what you believe, regardless of what others say?**

   a) Yes (2)
   b) No (1)

2. **Do others accept the most of your decisions?**

   a) Yes (2)
   b) No (1)

3. **Do prefer you to bear a 'daring' label?**

   a) Yes (2)
   b) No (1)

SELF ASSESSMENT RESULTS

3 points

Unfortunately, you probably feel embarrassed to become visible or stand out from the crowd. You are much nicer and polite in joining the masses, than to oppose the crowd in anything. The consequence of this state of affairs can be the fact that all your life, you will conduct yourself just like the majority of people around you — as part of the grey mass. If you do not like this prospect, we recommend you read this book through and carefully consider all practical tasks.

4–5 points

Not Bad! You are doing everything possible to live a conscious life and not become part of the crowd — the grey mass. Sometimes the fear of not being like everyone else, still scares you and keeps you from taking bold steps and decisions. To get rid of it and live your life more consciously, never for a moment ceasing to be IN THE HERE AND NOW, it is recommended to read this book until the end.

6 points

Excellent! You have a reluctance to be like everyone else — not likely to be part of the grey mass. You are good at independent judgment and are able to go your own way regardless of public opinion. Perhaps your behavior may seem strange or crazy to some people, but such is the fate of all people who dare to live consciously. People around you need communication with you to brighten up their grey existence. Paint their lives!

RECOMMENDATIONS ON CARRYING OUT THE PRACTICAL TASKS

1. ATTENTION! The practical tasks listed after each Chapter are not just for reading; you need them. With my years of experience with people, I know that oftentimes, people perform these tasks just 'to tick the box', as if in school; but this is your life, this is for you, take the assignments seriously.

2. For maximum results we recommend you perform the tasks within 24 hours, otherwise, leaving them for later, you are distancing yourself from your destiny and your success.

3. To answer all the questions, work out the practical tasks in a serene and tranquil environment. Find a quiet place where no one will be able to interfere; perhaps a time when no one is at home; or at night when everyone is asleep.

4. Be sure to reflect on the previous Chapter and go over all the items which you emphasized for yourself. Remember the decisions you made and write down your subsequent actions.

5. Certainly put specific time deadlines planned, and define restrictions which you will apply in relation to yourself; it will help you not to shelve implementation of the decisions you made.

6. Find someone to whom you could be accountable regarding your decisions, who could remind you of them — a kind of partner in working on yourself.

PRACTICAL TASKS

1. How do you assess the degree of 'awakeness' of your life? How consciously do you live? To what extent are you a reasoning man, and to what extent do you live by instincts and reflexes, that is, actually live the life of animals?

2. To what extent are you a part of the crowd — the grey mass? What percentage of your life do you live in 'automation' like a machine?

3. Assess how the statement of Benjamin Franklin applies to you: *"Many people die at the age of 25, and are only put in the grave at 75"*. Are you actively implementing a life-purpose or are you merely existing — in other words already 'dead'?

4. How often does this principle manifest in your life — *"THE BAD HEAD DOES NOT GIVE REST TO THE FEET"*? What do you intend to do in order to reduce the effect of this principle to a minimum?

CHAPTER 3

NOT BEING IN THE HERE AND NOW CAN LEAD TO SCHIZOPHRENIA

Schizophrenia — a disease, associated with the disintegration of thought processes.

The shift work of a team of psychiatrists was interrupted by a phone call. A doctor lifted the receiver and heard the following, "I just spoke to a woman who reported that her husband, as it turned out was Barack Obama. She reported that her husband worried about the global economic crisis, so much so that he could no longer sleep. The wife, as much as she could, tried to calm him down, "... they say, you are not to blame". The husband listened, then swung his head, unexpectedly he grew gloomy, and then declared, "No! This cannot continue; something must be done about this. As the president, I feel the enormous responsibility for the destinies of the planet!"

When his wife gently objected that the President is in fact, on the TV, she said that he compelled her to be saying that, in actual fact, he is Barack Obama, and here is an unofficial, but very friendly incognito, "But now it's time to operate openly, firmly and effectively — it's time to unite with Russia!"

The wife was very interested in such a prospect, and needed clarification on whether there were no negotiations with the Russian president — she had nothing to contribute to that regard. The husband replied that once the policy had reached a deadlock, then there was urgent need to restore order in the Senate — for which, with a hammer in his underpants, he decided to go to America on foot. In his opinion, the map, the direction and the distance was nothing. With the hammer, the Senate would be located! And that was it.

Of course, in order to prevent an international scandal, the man was already wanted by the team of medics. Apparently, the nearest police patrol would detain on the streets any man in shorts and with hammer in hand. 'Mr. President,' on 'business trip' was already being awaited in a serious state institution.

It would be laughable, if it weren't so sad. Maybe you personally have not encountered such cases, but certainly from time to time, you have heard about such incidents. What is the reason of such behavior from people who from time to time have been or, at least, seemed quite adequate, healthy and like everyone else, lived somewhere, had jobs, were married and raised children?

Schizophrenia (from the Greek: σχίζω — to split, and φρήν — mind) is a group of mental disorders that are associated with the disintegration of thought processes and emotional reactions. In other words, schizophrenic disorders are characterized by fundamental disturbances of thought and perception. The medical faculty of Stanford University describes schizophrenia as *"Thought disorder: a brain disorder that affects a person's ability to think clearly, manage emotions, make decisions, and relationships with others"*.

This brings to mind the statement of the famous scientist and inventor in the field of electrical and radio engineering, engineer, physicist Nikola Tesla (1856–1943): *"Modern scholars think deeply instead of thinking clearly. One must be sane to think clearly, but one can think deeply and be quite insane"*. I think these words are relevant not only to scientists, but to everyone. It is important to think deeply, but how often do we all meet people who look clever, so immersed in the solution of completely useless problems — and all because of the lack of clarity of thought. That is why it is so important to think clearly — this will help avoid further problems or even eliminate the problem at the very beginning of its occurrence.

Schizophrenia is characterized by:
- Psychosis — **a loss of contact with reality**
- Hallucinations — **false perceptions**
- Delusions — **false beliefs**
- **Deterioration of concentration**

All this is due to the fact that the person is systematically absent from HERE AND NOW.

SUPERFICIALITY AND IRRESPONSIBILITY — THE FIRST SIGNS OF SCHIZOPHRENIA

Elena has already made five attempts of suicide. This is repeated over and over again — when confronted with certain difficulties she swallows a handful of sleeping pills. After a long stay in intensive care unit, by the direction of a psychiatrist, she came to the psychologist who is puzzled — "If Elena is mentally healthy, then why has she already tried to kill herself for the fifth time?"

Elena, aged 25, graduated from College and had worked as a teacher in a kindergarten. She has two children, but is divorced from her husband. Her appearance could be the envy of any actress or pop star; beautiful shape, expressive facial features, big eyes — the only thing that gives away her unstable psychological state is her being sort of unkempt, not well-groomed or careless — her hair is dishevelled, the eye-pencil carelessly applied, even the dressing gown was unstitched along the seam.

Elena is sitting motionless at the reception of a psychologist, staring into the void. Her whole posture radiates indifference and serenity. Mind blank and distant, not even a hint of a glimmer of thought! Written all over Elena's face is the fact that people should never bother their heads to think.

The woman answers the psychologist's questions shortly and formally, superficially smiling as she mentions how she swallowed the tablets. It becomes clear that she always thoughtlessly reacts to everything that is unpleasant to her — either abuses the offender so that the offender runs to escape from her or if that first option fails, she then seizes the children, takes them away to her mother, then locks herself and . . . makes an attempt to fall asleep forever.

Questions about her little daughters brought her back to life — her face beaming. It turns out that she took the daughters to the mother so as not to harm them or make them scared. But to the question "Did you ever reflect over what would happen to them if you failed to recover?" "No" she answered, "I would be so stressed that I wouldn't think about anything."

When the psychologist tried to paint a picture of Elena's abandonment of her daughters, who are 2 and 3 years old, with tears in her eyes, she said she loves them, but never bothered to think about their future!

As you can see from this story, Elena's thinking bears the seal of **superficiality and frivolity.** She never thought about the fate of her children, about why she is responding this way and not otherwise. Elena had not considered the consequences of her actions that might be waiting in the future of her children. She looked at things so superficially and reacted as prompted by her feelings — when she hurts, then she either attacks or runs away. But even in her defence, she tries to shift the responsibility to someone else — *"I will go to sleep, and things will sort themselves out."*

Elena thoughtlessly responded to everything that was somehow unpleasant. How often do you react in this way, dear reader? Her thoughts were not subject to any one plan, and consequently became chaotic and unproductive. As a result, Elena's behavior became **irresponsible.** She was ready to condemn her children to the orphanage, but would not face the reality of solving her problems. Mindlessness and purely emotional reaction to, and withdrawal from a psychological difficulty (even escaping through death) are the reasons for repeated attempts of suicide by this young woman.

Superficiality

Superficiality, is the quality of a person with the tendency to be primitive, shallow and apparently in a hurry to perceive the world around us. A man with a superficial way of thinking does not go deep into the heart of any matter or issue, but seeks to simplify everything, reacting to situations quickly without initially reflecting over his or other people's words and actions. Such a person does not worry about performing any role assigned to them qualitatively. He lives a life of frivolity and lacks being HERE AND NOW. Superficial people pay no attention to what they hear, see or read, so they simply believe everything the media says without taking the trouble to query and analyse any information they receive, to be IN THE HERE AND NOW.

The English Explanatory Dictionary gives the meaning of the word 'surface' as 'a superficial aspect as opposed to the real nature of something'. It is the inattentiveness or superficial relation to something or an external acquaintance with something, without penetration into the main point. Synonymous with superficiality include: shallowness, frivolousness, lightness, lightheartedness (Thesaurus.com).

The reason for the problems that we talked about in the first chapter, such as:

- Forgetfulness
- Distraction
- The absence or weak degree of perseverance

— is that people do not try to grasp the essence of the information; they are superficial.

Superficiality can be inherent knowledge, but this does not automatically mean understanding, since 'surface' people are not accustomed to thinking deeply, reflecting and analysing. Unfortunately, superficiality is a world-wide disease of of our world today. To eradicate this vice in itself, I recommend you carefully examine my book — *'Why respect chess players or How to learn to think?'* Superficiality is the first sign that testifies that the person is not HERE AND NOW.

Irresponsibility

The second ominous sign of a mental disorder, fraught with such disease as schizophrenia, is irresponsibility. And although this quality is comfortable for the person himself, but for others, irresponsibility is the source of trouble and problems. Typical examples of irresponsibility are the following:

- The habit of relying on chance
- Postpone everything to a later time
- Do not think about the future

To the question "Did you do it or not?" The responsible person responds honestly, and in case of a positive answer, is ready to take the responsibility that is face the consequences, for example the payment of a fine. An irresponsible person runs away from his responsibility, strongly avoiding the answer to this question.

According to Thesaurus.com, the synonyms of 'irresponsibility' include: indiscretion, irrationality, silliness. Irresponsibility (the absence of a responsible attitude to life) is the position of a person who prefers the absence of targets and commitments, the unwillingness and inability to be responsible for the consequences of their own actions. Irresponsible people are actually adult children who are used to the fact that everything in life happens 'by itself'. Such people place excessive demands and claims against people and they never do what they are supposed to do.

In other words, irresponsibility is:

- Infantile living position
- Inability to make decisions
- Unwillingness to take responsibility for one's actions
- Inability to live in the adult world
- A way to conceal one's own laziness

Irresponsibility finds expression in unwillingness to make decisions in difficult situations. Such position is convenient for the person, as it relieves him of excess problems and efforts, but it is extremely destructive for his environment and society. Irresponsibility starts during the course of personality formation while the individual is under the influence of, first of all, parents. Parent 'gendarmes', 'rescuers' and 'tolerators' are especially dangerous to children. Children under such parents are at risk of immaturity as adults — not having acquired responsibility.

IRRESPONSIBILITY IS AN ATTEMPT OF THE PERSON TO ESCAPE FROM REALITY.

Schizophrenia is characterized by the fact that **the person has violated the sense of reality — in fact, he lives in his own world**. As you can see, they are at risk of becoming diagnosed with the strangeness of thought and behaviour, starting with, at first glance, 'harmless' things like superficiality and irresponsibility. Too often, ignoring the HERE AND NOW principle makes one:

- to first and foremost, escape from the reality
- then, to start denying it
- and then, to begin living in a self-made reality, completely ignoring the present reality

The danger of this state and behavior is evident. It all starts with the fact that the person is not HERE AND NOW.

SCHIZOPHRENIA IS AN ANTI-SOCIAL PERSONALITY DISORDER

Schizophrenia is also among the anti-social personality disorders, which can be characterized by lack of respect for the rights of others and failure to comply with social norms. When a person does not live HERE AND NOW in every moment of his existence, the following things begin to show in his life: he lacks empathy and is, as a rule, callous, cynical and contemptuous to the feelings, rights, and suffering of other people. Such people are usually unable to work with or maintain relationships with others. Approximately one in ten people diagnosed with schizophrenia commits suicide. What leads to such serious consequences, begins with harmless signs at first glance, such as:

- a self-focused life

- self-pity

Let's go back to our story of Elena, a woman so immersed in her own problems and was so focused on herself that even a psychologist found it hard to bring her out of this state: she lived in her own world, preferring to 'switch off', just to avoid having to be IN THE HERE AND NOW. This young woman also allowed herself to be so submerged in self-pity to the extent that committing suicide was the only way out of the situation. Let's see how the story ended.

Before releasing Elena from the office, the psychologist gave her a task designed to stir up her cogitative activity. The doctor instructed Elena to understand, remember and write down, who among the women in her room was friendlier and closer to her, which of the nurses was nice to her and who was less nice and again, she would need to justify and explain exactly why. These exercises would develop a person's ability to observe and record their thoughts, images, trends in events, even with the most unpleasant people.

Strangely enough, from this task Elena came alive, she found it interesting to answer to the posed questions. Previously, she constantly quarrelled with a grumpy nurse, but now, thanks to the psychological help, Elena learned to achieve such a turn of affairs, that even 'the old grumbler' was contented with it. Thus, the woman learned to control the situation, which improved her emotional skills and gave a positive result.

At once Elena rushed to the psychologist with the good news, "It worked! That nurse that previously only grumbled, told me: "So you see, the girl is good, are you feigning ignorance?"

Elena kept in touch with the psychologist after the discharge. At one point she said, "And how could I have lived like that before — without thinking? ... As if in a dream! Strange. Now, here I go, I feel, I understand, I can control myself. Sometimes I get frustrated, but at least I can now retroactively ponder why I broke down. And I could have died without knowing how to live! The horror! Never again will it ever happen.". Many years later, Elena is one of the most interesting and favorite teachers of Russian language and literature in one of the rural schools. In one of her lessons, she teaches children what she learned herself, thanks to her hard life-lesson, to THINK.

This story has a positive ending. To every person who is still, for the most part, not HERE AND NOW because of their superficiality or lack of responsibility, comes self-centredness or self-pity out of their dead-end life. Just like Elena realised this and began to really understand life, such people can begin to think and to be IN THE HERE AND NOW every second of their existence.

Finally, let's look at self-centredness and self-pity, what they are, their dangers and how to get rid of them.

SELF-CENTEREDNESS

To be self-centred means to become the egoist who is interested in others only so far as they have something of benefit. A person's expressions of egoism are in the form of: *"I, me, and mine, my interests. Everything that I want, I have to have at all costs"*. When our entire life revolves around ourselves, when self-admiration dominates and all attention is concentrated only on ourselves, then there is self-centeredness. Egoism or self-love generates pride. Pride doesn't allow one to discern the gifts and talents of others, to rejoice in their victories and progress. Arrogance and haughtiness make people appreciate only their own gifts and abilities. According to Fr. Alexander Elchaninov, the priest of the Russian Orthodox Church in Paris, *"Pride, vanity, conceit, haughtiness, arrogance, self-love — all are different manifestations of the same underlying phenomena — self-centredness"*.

Such a person does not see merit in others, he is one-sided and superficial. Self-centeredness in man strikes his vital energy, feelings, mind, and spreads very deep, up to his reasoning;

- *Unwillingness to work selflessly* is a sign of the penetration of self-centredness into one's **vital energy**
- *Strong desire for possessions* is a sign of the penetration of self-centredness into one's **feelings**
- *Constant desire to justify themselves and their outlook on life* is a sign of the penetration of self-centredness into one's **mind.**
- *Pride of his knowledge* is a sign of penetration of self-centredness into one's **reasoning.**

Pride exalts only the individual. Selfish people appreciate themselves more than others; they connect everything with themselves and begin to live for themselves only. Their attitude is, *"My country is better, my city is better, my family is better, my friends are better ...than others."* Pride is also a manifestation of self-centredness. Self-centredness is evident when you compare yourself with others, demonstrating your superiority and importance. The Russian Priest — Fr Alexander Elchaninov once said, *"Focusing on one's self takes a man away from the world and from God; he is, so to speak, chopped off from a common trunk of worldview and turns into a chip twisted around in an empty space."* This weakness is treated easily and simply by just ceasing to be focused on only yourself and your problems. Realize that you are not the navel of the earth and the world must not revolve around you and solve only your problems. Therefore, a good antidote is transferring your focus from your darling self to other people — for sure there is someone out there who is in pain and suffering and needs your support and encouragement. As a minimum, each person needs to be noticed, appreciated and accepted, to be shown love, care and attention. Why don't you reach out to those who are in a worse position than you, and show them the warmth of your heart?

SELF-PITY

How I wish that all of us would know that self-pity doesn't lead to anything good, but most people subconsciously engage in it. Self-pity begins with egoism and focus on self and one's problems. Egocentrism compels one to place emphasis on oneself, which turns them into victims who say:

- "Life is so unfair to me!"
- "Why did this happen to me?"
- "Why do those who have hurt me, not get punished?"

When a person starts feeling sorry for himself saying, *"Oh, I'm miserable. Dad died, my mom got sick, the child is not enrolled in school, nobody understands me and I am not loved and accepted!"* — It is possible that all this is true but the attention of the person is so absorbed on himself that he doesn't notice anything else and can't see other people around him who are passing through the same or even worse problems. Focusing on oneself blinds the person — making him insensitive to the needs of others and his heightened attention on himself accepts only the signals of his own trouble.

When you are feeling sorry for yourself, you begin to look for the 'excuse' to convince yourself that you have no power over the problem. Having found such a reason (excuse), you settle for the fact that there is no need to bother yourself, because the situation won't change anyway. And for such a person, it does not matter that other people encountered the same problem and overcame it successfully. The person who allows self-pity to prevail in his life will have a priori assumptions about solutions; no solution works for him because he is 'so special'! Even when there appears to be hope that something can work out, such a person will dismiss it, principally because he is convinced that the solution will still not help. Whatever the 'garment' self-pity wears to disguise itself, it can still be easily recognized. The result of self-pity is inaction and thereby no results; problems are not solved, the desired result is not achieved. At the heart of self-pity is the confidence that if we do nothing, but simply take offence at destiny, then destiny would become ashamed, and something will change.

When a person's emotions blind him from seeing what is really important, his focus shifts. He may make the wrong choice at crucial moments, which then exerts a decisive influence on his life. If we allow resentment and frustration to take over, if we prefer to 'play the victim', it will lead us nowhere because self-pity tightly closes the path to any progress and change. The most important thing to understand in order to escape the grip of self-pity is that our life is 'an ocean' of processes that constantly surround us, and as long as we are alive, we will be surrounded by problems, conflicts, threats, demands, and other unpleasant situations. In each of those situations we must think and find a way out, instead of feeling sorry for ourselves.

As a curative medicine, I would like to offer you a mantra for the downtrodden from Osho. One way of working with offense is using its gain — bringing this to the extreme and ultimately to the point of absurdity. The Osho mantra fits this as aptly as can be. To enhance the effect, it is recommended to print it, stand before the mirror and with expression, read it until the symptoms of self-pity completely disappear, together with self-focus and its problems.

I'm such a big turkey, I cannot afford to have someone to act according to its nature, if I do not like. I'm such a big turkey that if someone said or did not as I expected — I will chasten him with his offense. Oh, let him see how important it is — my resentment, let him receive it as a punishment for his 'misconduct'. After all, I'm very, very important turkey!

I do not value my life. So I do not value my life that I do not feel sorry for wasting my valuable time on offense. I give up the moments of joy, moments of happiness, moments of playfulness, I'd give this a minute of offense. And I do not care that these frequent moments add up to hours, hours — in the days, the days — in the weeks and weeks — in months and months — years. I do not mind to spend years of my life in grievance — because I do not appreciate my live. I do not know how to look at myself.

I am very vulnerable. I'm so vulnerable that I have to protect my territory and to respond by insult to anyone who touched it. I'm going to hang on my forehead the sign 'Beware of Dog' and just let someone try her invisible! I am so poor, I could not find a drop of generosity — to forgive, a drop of self-irony — to laugh, a drop of generosity — not to notice, a drop of wisdom — not to cling to, a drop of love — to accept. After all, I'm very, very important turkey!

So, in this Chapter we have considered that the absence of a person from being IN THE HERE AND NOW can lead to a mental disorder such as schizophrenia, which is characterized by a disintegration of thought. We saw that the first signs of schizophrenia can seem harmless at first glance, then the phenomenon of superficiality and irresponsibility in attitudes and behavior. Also, such a deviation in the development of personality can provoke the focus on oneself, self interests and self-pity. In the next Chapter, dear reader, we will see what causes the reluctance to exercise your brain. Keep reading! Stay tuned!

GOLDEN NUGGETS

1. A person with a superficial way of thinking does not go deeply into the essence of any business or matter, seeks to simplify everything, does everything quickly, but on the 'surface', not reflecting over his or other people's words and actions, and not worrying about how to perform the role assigned to them qualitatively HERE AND NOW.

2. Irresponsibility is man's attempt to escape from reality.

3. Strangeness in thinking and behavior of man starts with things that look 'harmless' at first glance: behaviours such as superficiality and irresponsibility cause him to be at risk of a diagnosis of schizophrenia.

4. When a person does not live in the HERE AND NOW every moment of his existence, his personality undergoes changes that are usually classified as anti-social. It becomes difficult for him to get along and work with other people.

5. Anti-social disorders lead to self-focus and self-pity.

6. To be interested only in oneself (self-focus) means to be an egoist; one who is interested in others only so far as they have something of benefit to attract his attention.

7. *"Pride, vanity, self-love, haughtiness, arrogance, conceit — all are different manifestations of the same underlying phenomenon of self-centeredness"* — Fr Alexander Elchaninov

8. When a person's emotions blind him from seeing what is really important, his focus shifts. He may make the wrong choice at crucial moments, which then exerts a decisive influence on his life.

9. Self-pity closes the path to any changes.

SELF-ASSESSMENT

1. **How deeply do you investigate the essence of a phenomenon?**
   a) I am quite a superficial person (0)
   b) Many things escape my attention (1)
   c) I try to penetrate into everything deeply and thoroughly, but I do not always succeed (3)
   d) I am a very critical and meticulous person, I don't stop until I get to the heart of the matter (4)

2. **You live in the real world, you have no obsessions, unhealthy imaginations. From time to time, you can dream and dream, but you don't live in the world of imaginations.**
   a) This statement is completely untrue concerning me (0)
   b) It applies to me to a lesser extent (1)
   c) To a greater extent this applies to me (3)
   d) Absolutely (4)

3. **How often do you feel sorry for yourself?**
   a) Very often (0)
   b) Sometimes (1)
   c) Rarely (3)
   d) Never (4)

Self assessment results

0–3 points

Most likely, you are often haunted by the desire to escape from reality; you are not concerned about the consequences of your actions and deeds; you think little about what can cause superficial judgments and actions. Those deviations in personality, which can lead to these behaviors, are risky for your mental health. To try changing your approach to life, we recommend that you continue reading this book, carrying out all the assignments after studying all the recommendations for their implementation.

4–8 points

It is difficult for you to control your emotions and feelings when they arise, to delve into the essence of things and be a responsible person. You feel an acute need to become more adequate in expressing your feelings, but also more responsible and meticulous. In this case, you will be further assisted by reading through this book and performing all the practical tasks at the end of each Chapter.

9–12 points

Congratulations! Given the opportunity, you try not to escape from reality. You indulge only in constructive dreams that have a specific deadline for implementation. You are ready to become the one who can share your healthy vision of the world with other people, be sure to make it!

RECOMMENDATIONS
ON CARRYING OUT THE
PRACTICAL TASKS

1. ATTENTION! The practical tasks listed after each Chapter are not just for reading; you need them. With my years of experience with people, I know that oftentimes, people perform these tasks just 'to tick the box', as if in school; but this is your life, this is for you, take the assignments seriously.

2. For maximum results we recommend you perform the tasks within 24 hours, otherwise, leaving them for later, you are distancing yourself from your destiny and your success.

3. To answer all the questions, work out the practical tasks in a serene and tranquil environment. Find a quiet place where no one will be able to interfere; perhaps a time when no one is at home; or at night when everyone is asleep.

4. Be sure to reflect on the previous Chapter and go over all the items which you emphasized for yourself. Remember the decisions you made and write down your subsequent actions.

5. Certainly put specific time deadlines planned, and define restrictions which you will apply in relation to yourself; it will help you not to shelve implementation of the decisions you made.

6. Find someone to whom you could be accountable regarding your decisions, who could remind you of them — a kind of partner in working on yourself.

PRACTICAL TASKS

1. Analyze how superficial you are. How deeply do you delve into the essence of things happening around you? Give yourself a score on a 10-point scale, where 0 is the minimum, 10 — maximum. Make a plan for the development of rigorous attitude to your life, full of attention to details.

2. Analyze how irresponsible you are. How much of a mature and responsible attitude do you lack in your life? Give yourself a score on a 10-point scale, where 0 is the minimum, 10 — maximum. Make a plan of action for the elimination of irresponsibility in your life.

3. Analyze your level of self-centeredness. To what extent has the focus of your attention shifted to yourself? Give yourself a score on 10-point scale, where 0 is the minimum, 10 — maximum. Make a plan of action to improve your worldview on life, yourself and others.

4. Analyze the level of self-pity that you experience. How much is your sensitivity shifted to focus on yourself? Give yourself a score on 10-point scale, where 0 is the minimum, 10 — maximum. Make a plan of action to improve your worldview on life, yourself and others.

CHAPTER 4

WHAT CAUSES AN UNWILLINGNESS TO EXERCISE THE BRAIN

In the previous Chapter we saw how the absence of the person in the HERE AND NOW has a high probability of leading to a mental illness such as schizophrenia, which is characterized by the decay of thinking. We also learned that the first signs of schizophrenia may be innocuous at first glance, things like superficiality and irresponsibility. We found that schizophrenia results in focusing on self and the increased feeling of self-pity. In this Chapter we will look at what causes reluctance to exercise the brain.

NOT BEING IN THE HERE AND NOW IS A CAUSE FOR ALARM

Imagine you were alone in a small Chinese village. You neither understand the language of the people nor what's written around you — advertisements on poles, price tags in the stores, restaurant menus, street signs, placards of the transport systems and so on. The prevailing custom seems strange to you and the actions that the natives so easily perform (e.g. eating with chopsticks), look complex. As if this were not enough, everybody's attention is on you. Funny thing is, they address you as if they were long-time and well acquainted with you.

An event like this makes one feel as if they had some serious memory disorder. What could be worse: losing memory, forgetting one's name, one's past, the faces of loved ones? It all starts with a minor breach of the memory of recent events that can be seen only by means of close observation. Gradually 'forgetfulness' is strengthened, memory begins to fail and facts from the past disappear from the entire segments of memory. Then one starts losing the sense of place and time, simultaneously losing common sense and becoming critical of things. Possible changes in behavior can set in; the person becomes indifferent to everything, has an attack of aggression, there are uncontrollable desires, the person falls back into childhood. Over several years, comes complete mental and physical disintegration of the personality, which is accompanied by incontinence of urine and stool. The ending is death from starvation or infection — this puts an end to the terrible suffering of the patient and his loved ones.

All these are symptoms of Alzheimer's disease[1], an incurable degenerative disease of the Central nervous system characterized by progressive loss of mental abilities (memory, language, logical thinking). Alzheimer's disease is the most common cause of dementia in elderly and senile age, the share of this disease accounts for 60–70% of all cases of loss or deterioration of memory at this age. There will be 1 million people with dementia in the UK by 2025. An

---

1   Degenerative signs of destruction of cells and/or organs.

estimated 5.4 million Americans of all ages have Alzheimer's disease in 2016. Of the 5.4 million Americans with Alzheimer's, an estimated 5.2 million people are age 65 and older, and approximately 200,000 individuals are under age 65 (younger-onset Alzheimer's).

In Ukraine alone, Alzheimer's disease affects more than a million people. By 2020, according to forecasts, the number of such patients will increase by 28%. The first symptoms of Alzheimer's disease may appear between the age of 40 and 70, the incidence is as high as 30%.

Dementia is a syndrome in which there is degradation of not only memory, but also the thinking, behaviour and ability to perform normal daily activities. Although this disease affects mostly older people, it is not a normal part of aging. Dementia is one of the major causes of disability and dependency among older people around the world. It can undermine both physical and psychological health of those people who are caring for the sick. Family and society in general suffer socially and economically from this disease.

Worldwide, 35.6 million people have dementia, and more than half (58%) of them live in low and middle income. Every year there are 7.7 million new cases of the disease. Estimated proportion of the general population aged 60 years and older with dementia at any moment in time is from 2 to 8 people for every 100 people. According to forecasts, the total number of people with dementia will double every 20 years, to 65.7 million in 2030 and 115.4 million in 2050.

This disease is more common among uneducated people in unskilled professions. A person with high intelligence is less likely to encounter manifestations of Alzheimer's disease for the reason that there is a greater number of connections between the nerve cells. This means that at the death of some cells, lost functions can be transferred to other cells not previously involved.

It is interesting that complaints from younger people include: the inability to concentrate, most familiar words disappearing off the head and very important meetings being forgotten. The same applies to even 25–30 year-olds who are active, successful and goal-oriented people; they too complain about the inability to concentrate, forgetfulness, absent-mindedness. And it doesn't bother us!

THE REASON THAT THERE IS A DISINTEGRATION OF THE PERSONALITY AND ABILITIES OF THE PERSON, IS THAT PEOPLE DON'T LIKE TO EXERCISE THEIR BRAIN. Thus, such people can bring in their old age, the unwanted baggage of dementia (senile dementia, or colloquially — senile insanity), Alzheimer's, etc. So it is important to always be IN THE HERE AND NOW. **If from a young age people have not developed the habit of concentrating and keeping focused, then the probability of the Alzheimer's disease, one of the most common causes of dementia and senility in elderly age, increases several times.** Whether you will add to the number of patients with this illness largely depends on you, dear reader.

BEING IN THE HERE AND NOW IS A NECESSITY FOR OUR BRAIN

Contemplation without thinking tires.
When I have no more and more new
ideasfor processing, I just become sick.
CENTURY GOETHE

So, we have found that **people who have not learned to concentrate and focus while in their youth, may experience lapses in memory in old age.** To avoid this, you need to connect all of your senses to listen and hear 100% — to always be IN THE HERE AND NOW, and also to put your brain to work.

Many parts of the body require constant care and training. This primarily concerns the muscles of the body — if they are trained, the person can easily lift a weight of at least 120 kg, exceeding his own weight. But if muscles are used rarely, they can either atrophy or become unable to cope with given load; it becomes difficult to lift anything of significant weight or even to climb stairs for multiple floors.

The astronauts, for example used to contend with many adverse effects of weightlessness, one of which was the rapid atrophy of the muscles and the subsequent reduction of all physical characteristics of the body. To solve this problem, special simulators were installed on space stations in which astronauts are simply compelled to be engaged just a few hours a day, as this is vital. Here is what cosmonaut Alexander Lazutkin, who spent more than six months (184 days 22 hours) at the station "Mir", said in an interview:

Question: What was the most difficult thing
for you in the everyday life while in space?

> Answer: *For me personally, it was difficult to engage
> in physical activity. Despite the fact that I
> am the master of gymnastic sports, that is
> to say that I am a savvy person, it was as
> hard to force myself to engage in physical
> exercise. Because there is a feeling that the
> body resists physical education. It enjoys this
> weightlessness. Muscles are happy that they
> do not need to work, and they do not want
> to work. That is the reason I struggled with
> myself.*

Question: But you still continued to
engage in physical activity?

> Answer: *Yes of course, it is vitally important. Firstly,
> the muscles will continue to atrophy, since
> the situation is already bad. Secondly, it is
> possible to forget about the return to Earth,
> because after returning with such atrophied
> muscles, you will not be able to live — the
> cardiovascular system fails, the muscles will
> not be able to support you. In general, you
> will be invalid. In other to function upon
> return to Earth, it is necessary to engage in
> physical exercises while in space.*

As you can see, exercise is vital for our muscles. Without it, it's difficult to sustain life in your body. However, we can apply this parallel to the human brain. What will happen to our mental capabilities if we have not developed the habit of straining our minds? The need for straining is not only applicable to muscles in the arms and legs but to the brain too; the brain needs exercise. It needs a 'new' food for thought, fresh ideas, the ability to solve complex problems and finding answers to questions. Only in this case will the grey matter not experience stagnation, but operate at 100% capacity.

The brain is a unique organ in the human body, the importance of which can hardly be overestimated. It coordinates the activities of all body systems. The basic cognitive[2] or informative functions of the brain include:

- Memory
- Attention
- Thinking

The human brain consists of billions of nerve cells, each of which produces and receives messages from other nerve cells. At the end of the nerve cells are neurotransmitters — types of chemicals through which messages are transmitted from one nerve cell to another organ. In the human brain with a diagnosis of 'schizophrenia', the above messaging system is not working properly. The cognitive abilities of such a person are reduced — an example of which is poor concentration. HOW WELL WE REMEMBER AND HOW FAST WE THINK, LARGELY DEPENDS ON THE CONDITION OF OUR BRAIN.

Therefore to help maintain the tone of the functioning of this vital organ, training is vital for the brain. It was rel-

---

2   Cognitive activities — as a result of which a person comes to a definite decision and/or knowledge, that is, intellectual activity, which leads to understanding (interpretation) of something

atively recently believed that the properties of the human brain formed by the time of adulthood are not amenable to improvement. However, by the end of the twentieth century, scientists have confirmed the plasticity of the brain and its incredible ability to adapt. Experimentally, it has been proven that the human brain is constantly changing in response to changes in the external environment. This means that, **regardless of age, the cognitive brain function can be improved.**

Therefore there is the need to train cognitive activity throughout life. This means that throughout life, each of us has something to continue to learn and innovate, discovering hitherto unknowns — whether it be learning foreign languages, cooking, computer, craft, dance, etc. THE MORE ACTIVE AND DIVERSE A PERSON'S MENTAL ACTIVITY, THE MORE LIKELY HE WOULD LIVE HIS WHOLE LIFE WITH A SOUND MIND AND MEMORY.

The human brain is designed in such a way that it starts to deteriorate when not being used. Just as any car would rust three times faster when parked in the garage than if it were intensively being used on the roads, the same applies to the possession of any foreign language: for example, to know Chinese, you must speak it, even a little, but every day. The higher the activity of the brain, the more it draws into itself oxygen-enriched blood. It is known that the MORE a PERSON EXERCISES HIS BRAIN, THE MORE NEURAL CONNECTIONS ARE FORMED. And on this information network depends both intellectual and mental health. If the man makes little use of his brain, the existing neural connections are weak, so that the brain receives less oxygen, and deteriorates. So the information neural network of the brain can and needs to be exercised, because every new irritation contributes to the emergence of new relations, and this process does not depend on a person's age.

When it comes to activating the cognitive processes of the cerebral cortex by fresh impressions, there is no dependency on one's age. The only difference is that during childhood, adolescence and youth, coupled with the learning in school and College, the curiosity factor consistently provides the brain with fresh impressions. But over the years, routine[3], in the worst sense of the word, begins to dominate human perception. Therefore, IT IS IMPORTANT TO ACQUIRE THE SKILLS OF THINKING THROUGHOUT LIFE, TO LEARN TO SOLVE PROBLEMS IN NEW WAYS, TO APPLY A NEW APPROACH TO EVERYTHING YOU DO.

What does it mean to train the brain? The brain, like the muscles, changes its properties and may enhance their functions depending on the quantity and quality of the exercise done. Importantly, **the active brain postpones aging and allows a person to be IN THE HERE AND NOW, not even momentarily 'dropping' out of this state.** People who don't like to strain their brains for mental work, considerably age quicker. The brain needs to be trained as well as muscles. The more trained our brain becomes, the more extended its capabilities.

---

3   Routine — following the usual pattern, which turned into a mechanical habit, when it begins to dominate the inertia — the tendency to do something familiar, immunity to the new, progressive retardation.

Thus, if a person does not learn the art of being HERE AND NOW, if he doesn't develop the habit of concentration and focus, the likelihood of Alzheimer's disease, one of the most common causes of dementia in elderly and senile age, increases several times. RELUCTANCE TO EXERCISE THE BRAIN ACCELERATES AGING AND CAUSES MENTAL DISORDERS IN OLD AGE.

SIX PILLARS OF INTELLECTUAL LONGEVITY

If a person, for most of the time isn't HERE AND NOW, such way of life can lead to Alzheimer's disease. To prevent dementia experts advise people in old age to be socially active and to lead an active intellectual life. The more active the person is, the more he is involved in public life (activities of public organizations, charities, and so on), the more opportunities his brain has to compensate for those functions that can be affected by the onset of old age.

What does it mean to lead an active intellectual life? Let's examine it more closely. So, our mental activity rests on the following six pillars:

1. **Say "Yes" to life.** Without such an attitude towards life, the dream of extending mental longevity becomes impossible. The more often the word 'no' is said, the more likely it is that life-denying 'programs' sit inside the person, and it affects the functioning of both the brain and other parts of the human body. One of the characteristics of people living a full and long life is that they are more likely to say "Yes" to new ideas, willingness to take a risk

or try something new. Take for example, the famous billionaire, Richard Branson, whose subordinates prefer to call "Mr. Yes". This is because his response to any proposal is "Yes". Optimistic and cheerful people more often say "Yes" than "No", they are open to any new suggestions from friends, relatives and partners.

2. **Thirst for knowledge.** Throughout life, you must be curious and never be afraid to experiment. THE LOW LEVEL OF EDUCATION IS AN INDIRECT RISK FACTOR FOR DEVELOPING ALZHEIMER'S DISEASE. *"I would not say that education can protect us, but educational training and mental work, of course, prolongs the life of a sick person"*, said a senior researcher at the Department of mental pathology of the elderly, the Moscow research Institute of psychiatry, Oleg Smirnov. He recommends people to keep active in the community for as long as possible, *"The longer a person is active physically and mentally, the longer the memory retains attention and other features to confront this disease"*, the doctor said.

3. **Train your memory.** Find and memorize new information that compels your head to work. Researcher Arthur Kramer, a professor of psychology at the University of Illinois, found that when people aged 58-78 years, leading mainly sedentary lifestyle, start to walk for several hours a day, their attention is amplified several times. The same applies to the training of the mind: the more

you solve riddles, crossword puzzles, learn more poetry, the more attentive and concentrated you'll be on your work.

4. **Humour and calm.** Connect youthful recklessness with the maturity and wisdom of age, get such pleasure from life, never allow sadness to get the best of you. There is a wise saying, by which we can be guided in life: *"Do not take the bad into your head and the heavy into your hands"*. We can tire ourselves out in desperate situations if we complicate everything and inflate them to incredible proportions. In English there is a rule of three 'don'ts': *"Don't carry, don't worry, don't hurry"* — implying that "Don't carry heavy weights, don't worry about them, don't hurry to escape them".

There are always things that we cannot change, so by worrying about them we are only making things worse for ourselves. A German theologian Karl Friedrich Ettinger (1702–1782) once said, *"God, grant me the serenity to accept the things I cannot change, courage to change the things I can and wisdom to know the difference."* In references, quotations and sayings of Anglo-Saxon countries this quote is attributed to American theologian Reinhold Niebuhr (1892–1971). With this approach to life, I believe, you'll be able to keep the humor and calm, no matter what.

5. **Contacts and communication.** Maintain friendships and always look for new contacts. Do not allow yourself to withdraw into solitude. Be interested in the people around you. American scientists in David Geffen School of Medicine examined the cells of

people who live in so-called social exclusion — that is, alone. The experiment showed that a lonely life is associated with changes in the activity of genes that are responsible for the inflammation of the body, which leads to a weakening of the immune system and increases the risk of viral infections, cancer and cardiovascular diseases. Genes in leukocytes of lonely people mutate and lead to failure of the protective functioning of the immune system that are designed to repulse all sorts of viruses.

When a person begins to communicate to friends and acquaintances, (and for each person it is very important to feel needed), the problem of loneliness and social isolation goes away by itself. An active social life begins.

6. **Find the meaning of life.** Only the life that is lived for the sake of its goal has full meaning. Neither children nor family, nor any of the achievements like planting a tree, building a house and raising a son and so on, are really the divine meaning of any human life. Each person has a *'personal meaning of life, converted into a practical purpose'*. According to the dictionary *'Psychology and characterology concepts'*, we are talking about the vocation or calling of a person — *"the original plan and reason for the existence of an object; the ultimate goal of existence of the subject"* (Myles Monroe — business consultant, author of several bestsellers dedicated to leadership, personal growth and spiritual development). Mental longevity is impossible without finding the afore-mentioned.

Albert Einstein (1879–1955), theoretical physicist, one of the founders of modern theoretical physics, Nobel Prize in physics in 1921, a social activist and humanist, gives the following advice: *"Strive not in order to succeed, but to make your life meaningful"*.

FIVE EASY WAYS TO TRAIN YOUR BRAIN

Now, earlier we talked to you, dear reader, that many of us regularly exercise just to maintain our body in good shape. But it is not only the muscles that require regular training. Neural pathways and connections in the brain should also get their training 'dosage'. How can this be done?

Let me remind you that there are five main cognitive functions:

1. Memory
2. Attention
3. Language
4. Visual-spatial skills
5. Reasoning

To maintain the health of the brain in optimal shape, it is very important to stimulate all five areas. Here are five simple exercises you can do every day.

1. **Memory.** Memory plays a key role in all cognitive operations, whether it be reading, thinking or counting. We have several different types of memory, but we usually remember them only after they start failing. Actually, coaching the memory in order to keep it in good working condition is easy

enough. For example, trying to remember the words of previously unknown songs after listening to them, helps to stimulate the production of the chemical compounds that improve memory. A good exercise is trying to dress in complete darkness, using a different hand to brush your teeth, etc. This change in habitual patterns of behavior not only improves the already existing neural connections, but creates new ones as well.

2. **Attention.** Attention is necessary for us all the time; it helps us focus on the task at hand, despite all the distractions, or maintain parallel operation on several tasks. You can also encourage attention by simply changing the usual order of things — go to work using a new route or just rearranging things on your desktop. This will be enough to arouse your attention and get focused. Another effective exercise is to perform multiple tasks simultaneously. For example, listening to an audio book while jogging or bike-riding while carrying out some mental calculations.

3. **Language.** Here we should pay attention to the ability to recognize, remember and understand words. At the same time you can develop grammatical skills and to expand your vocabulary. For this you simply need to read, and read something that you usually do not read. For example, if you are mainly interested in sports, try reading a little bit about financial analysis or popular science articles. New words are always easier to

understand in context, and if this does not work, then you can refer to dictionaries.

4. **Visual-spatial skills.** We live in a color three-dimensional world, and analysis of visual information is vital for correct interaction with the surrounding space. To develop visual-spatial skills, try to enter a room and look around. In order to remember five random items, go out of the room, and recall the five random items and where they are located. If you find that easy, then wait two hours and try to recall the items again. Try performing this exercise anytime and anywhere. Try to remember the location of items on your way to work, in your office or the hallway that you use a couple of times a day, etc.

5. **The reasoning.** Sometimes without realizing it, we use logic, conjecture and evaluate probability, reflect and make decisions every day. If you want to exercise your brain, then doing that will require you to calculate the strategy and the evaluation of possible consequences.

Let me remind you that the use of cognitive abilities and their training is no less important than physical activity. Learning about the five basic functions and their different ways of development and training enables you perform these exercises every day. This will help you to keep a sound mind for as long as possible.

Thus, in this Chapter we studied the consequence of a reluctance to exercise your brain. I think you clearly understand, dear reader, that reluctance to be IN THE HERE AND NOW carries disastrous consequences in old age, threatening diseases such as Alzheimer's disease and senile dementia could be some of them. We have learned with you in this Chapter that it is absolutely necessary to train our brain in a wide variety of mental activities. And the sooner we start this 'preventive' measure, the better for us and our mental longevity. Most importantly, for us to constantly remain useful, we necessarily need to be IN THE HERE AND NOW every moment of our lives. In the next Chapter we will talk about what it means to be IN THE HERE AND NOW and look at the advantages of this constant presence every second.

GOLDEN NUGGETS

1. The reason that many people in old age await the disintegration of personality and abilities (dementia), lies in the fact that people don't like to put their brains to work.

2. If a person does not develop the habit of concentrating and maintaining focus at young age, then the probability of the Alzheimer's disease, one of the most common causes of dementia in the elderly, increases several times.

3. People who have not learned to concentrate and focus while in their youth, may experience lapses in memory in old age.

4. Just as our muscles need regular exercise, our brain needs exercising too. It helps the brain to remain viable and productive for a longer time.

5. The more active and diverse the mental activity of a person, the more likely that he will live all his life with a sound mind and strong memory.

6. How well we remember things and the speed with which we think, in many respects depends on that state of our brain.

7. Regardless of age, the cognitive brain functions can be improved upon.

8. Working the brain postpones aging and allows a person to be IN THE HERE AND NOW, not 'dropping out' from this state, even for a moment.

9. Reluctance to exercise the brain accelerates aging and leads to mental disorders in old age.

SELF ASSESSMENT

1. **What type of labour occupies you at work?**

   a) Mental (2)

   b) Physical (1)

2. **What is your education?**

   a) Average (1)

   b) Higher (2)

3. **If you're already retired, or when you come to that stage, you want to:**

   a) Be inactive (1)

   b) Continue to work (2)

Self-assessment results

3 points

I'm sorry, but, apparently, you do not like to exercise your brain. This may cause a higher risk of problems with thinking and memory in old age, and perhaps even earlier. If you want to avoid this, we recommend you read this book to the end. This will allow you to change your attitude concerning this issue and take the necessary measures in time to avoid the Alzheimer's disease or dementia, as soon as you retire.

4–5 points

Not bad! You agree that there is need for longevity in the field of your thinking, attention and memory. Further reading and study of all practical tasks at the end of each Chapter will help you to improve on your efforts in car-

ing for the most important organ of the human body —
the brain.

6 points

Am excited for you! You understand perfectly well about
the need for maintaining an active life mentally. Therefore
you are taking all the necessary preventive measures to
avoid serious mental problems in old age. You still have a
lot to learn, I encourage you to share your experiences with
the people around you.

RECOMMENDATIONS ON CARRYING OUT THE PRACTICAL TASKS

1. ATTENTION! The practical tasks listed after each Chapter are not just for reading; you need them. With my years of experience with people, I know that oftentimes, people perform these tasks just 'to tick the box', as if in school; but this is your life, this is for you, take the assignments seriously.

2. For maximum results we recommend you perform the tasks within 24 hours, otherwise, leaving them for later, you are distancing yourself from your destiny and your success.

3. To answer all the questions, work out the practical tasks in a serene and tranquil environment. Find a quiet place where no one will be able to interfere; perhaps a time when no one is at home; or at night when everyone is asleep.

4. Be sure to reflect on the previous Chapter and go over all the items which you emphasized for yourself. Remember the decisions you made and write down your subsequent actions.

5. Certainly put specific time deadlines planned, and define restrictions which you will apply in relation to yourself; it will help you not to shelve implementation of the decisions you made.

6. Find someone to whom you could be accountable regarding your decisions, who could remind you of them — a kind of partner in working on yourself.

PRACTICAL TASKS

1. Find out about what has led to the frequent (and unsuccessful) searches for keys, the forgotten promises, the missed meetings, etc. Is there a need to see a specialist, or will a two-week holiday and good time-management improve things? Memory Lab Specialist at the Clinic for Nervous Diseases, A. Y. Kozhevnikov (MMA of I. M. Sechenov) suggests to check for the existence of the following symptoms:

   - You never remember what and where you placed things, and because of this, you keep losing things all the time.

   - You can't seem to remember the names and faces of people with whom you get acquainted.

   - You quickly forget what you just read or watched on TV.

   - Quite recently, you have lost interest in those things you used to love e.g. reading, watching movies or meeting people.

   - You forget how things are said during a conversation; it is often difficult to find the right words, you often stipulate.

   - It is often difficult for you to concentrate.

   - You have difficulty in counting the money in the safe.

- It is difficult for you to find the correct route in an unfamiliar part of the city independently

- Your co-workers and family members pay attention to your memory challenges.

If you have at least three items from the above list, which cause a significant inconvenience to you and your family for the last few weeks, it may make sense to consult a doctor.

2. What causes your unwillingness to exercise your brain? What will you do to avoid this?

3. Develop for yourself a program for exercising your brain to keep it in good working condition for as long as possible.

CHAPTER 5

HERE AND NOW — DEFINITION, CONCEPT, ADVANTAGES

Before moving on to the peak of our story, that for which all this writing is all about, let us recall what we have talked about in the previous chapter. In Chapter 4, we have discussed about *What causes the unwillingness to exercise the brain*, and we have come to the conclusion that the reluctance to put in the effort to be IN THE HERE AND NOW can lead to disastrous consequences such as Alzheimer's disease and senile dementia at old age. We have found that it is necessary to exercise the brain, and that the sooner we start the 'preventive' measure, the longer and more meaningful the quality of our life will be.

So, it's time to talk about what it means to be IN THE HERE AND NOW, what are the advantages of this absolute presence — HERE AND NOW. You'll even find that the ABILITY TO BE IN THE HERE AND NOW IS AVAILABLE TO ALL! Do you want to know how real this is? I invite you to continue reading!

WHAT IT MEANS TO BE IN THE HERE AND NOW

It was a Friday afternoon. The week drew to a close. It was the month of May, the air was full of summer smell of warm and upcoming troubles in the country. Antonina Petrovna was sitting at a meeting. The authorities somehow did not consider that it happened on the eve of the weekend, and gathered all the experts in order to take stock of the past week and plan for the future. In this regard, the people sat with their thoughts 'scattered' in the coming weekend. Antonina was not an exception.

Her beloved mum Valentine Kuzminichna has long been retired and therefore with the approach of the Summer moved to their country home in the village and remained there until the first frost. Antonina had not seen her mother for a while; the last time when she planned to do it, she was detained by other important issues — and therefore she felt she missed her mum. She had time to do much around the house, walk to the river with the family, fry kebabs, and therefore Antonina focused all her mental powers on what and in what order things needed to be done in the next few days.

Suddenly, like a thunderclap out of a clear sky came the voice of the boss, who tried to snatch her 'suspended animation', in which, unwittingly Antonina had fallen. She awoke, as it were, from sleep! She looked puzzled at Vasily Nikolaevich and colleagues, who all stared at her, waiting for an answer. The worst thing is that Antonina had not heard the question, and therefore could not answer. She had no choice but to mumble something unintelligible, that she accidentally zoned out, and asked the boss to repeat the questions put to her. The disapproving gaze from the boss and grin from colleagues made her understand that she was doing something wrong...

Have you, dear reader been in the same situation as Antonina Petrovna? Although her body was present in the meeting, in her thoughts she was at that time carried away to her mother at the cottage, in the village. She ceased to perceive what was happening around her at that moment. She was not concerned about anything that was said in the last few minutes; never heard what was said, even when the boss turned directly to her. Her reality was not what was happening at the meeting. Her reality was in the village, with her mother, who was waiting for her there, the potatoes that needed to be planted next weekend, etc. We can say unequivocally that Antonina Petrovna was not HERE AND NOW. What is this special state called HERE AND NOW?

HERE AND NOW is a state of consciousness in which all attention is focused on what is happening in this place and at this moment: not somewhere far away or someone, but HERE; not in the past or in the future, but NOW.

To be in the HERE AND NOW means:

- To be focused and concentrated
- To be observant
- To be able to focus the heart, thoughts, attention, mental energy in one direction
- To be purposeful
- Not to dwell on the past because it's already gone

- Not to live in the future, as it has not yet arrived
- To pay attention to the words:
  NOW, AT THIS MOMENT

INBETWEEN THE PAST AND FUTURE

If we focus on the past, we do not have enough energy for it. If we live in the future — we live in fantasies! The real time is only now! And it's here that the process of our change begins.
SOCRATES

HERE AND NOW is **impossible**, if we always:
- remain in our thoughts
- recall past events
- imagine the future
- think about faraway places

The one who constantly dwells in the HERE AND NOW is in reality, doing something significant even though it may not be much. Most people spend their lives 'digging up' the past or building 'castles' in the air. Such habits do not help us become effective in achieving present goals or to see the fulfilment of our dreams. It doesn't matter whether we are thinking about the events of many years ago or about what will happen in a week, it is rather costly when we fix our 'inner eyes' on the past or the future because we are being disconnected from HERE AND NOW, and our minds begin to wander away, drawn by memory and imagination. To be in the HERE AND NOW means that we are dealing with only what is happening or can happen now, without burdening ourselves with problems of the past or future that are not presently in our power to change. Even in difficult situations it makes sense to focus only on what can be solved HERE AND NOW.

It is important to remember that —

- What has already happened in the past was real only when it happened
- What will happen belongs to the future, it will be important when it does happen

To fully experience the present, it is necessary to take specific actions consciously and in order to live life consciously, it is important to be IN THE HERE AND NOW. And what is awareness? **Awareness** is a continuous tracking of current experiences; that is, a state in which one focuses on the experience of the present moment, trying not to be distracted by the events of the past or thinking about the future.

To fully experience the present, you must also pay attention to words like 'now', 'here' and 'in this moment'. The same must be true for anybody wherever they find themselves. But to live HERE AND NOW does not mean to live solely in the present, without worries, being blind and deaf to what we could learn from the past or ignoring what lies ahead. **Completely embracing the present also involves the awareness of the present reminders of past lessons and planning future actions, which allows us to properly and adequately act in the present.**

Socrates was right (see the epigraph to this subchapter), arguing that the process of change begins with acquiring the skill to be IN THE HERE AND NOW, without once again wasting the energy reflecting on the past or fantasizing about what will happen in the future. It is very important to live and abide in real time — the actual time in which we are right now.

THE BENEFITS OF BEING IN THE HERE AND NOW

Let's look at the advantages of having a 100 percent presence and involvement in what is happening right now. The ability to be IN THE HERE AND NOW, having a well-developed attention will enable you to:

- Quickly analyse the task
- Adequately capture its essence
- Navigate the situation easily, depending on changing conditions
- Discern what is important
- Take into note of any nuances
- Be prudent
- Retain the memory of the present events for a long period.

WHEN WE ARE ABLE TO FOCUS OUR THOUGHTS IN ONE DIRECTION AND ON ONE TASK, IT INCREASES THE SPEED AND EFFICIENCY OF PERFORMING THE TASK TEN TIMES.

"Any musician will confirm that at high concentration, you can accomplish in two hours rehearsal what will take six to eight hours in a more 'relaxed', that is defocused state," said Elena Grintsov, a professional musician, Director of the Percussion Ensemble, winner of the Ukraine Cabinet Ministers prize, a laureate of international and all-Ukrainian competitions, teacher-trainer, specialist of the highest category. She added, "Really, it is possible to be occupied six to eight hours, and simultaneously thinking about something else or not connecting all resources: emotional, physical... And it is possible to concentrate all the innate resources in one point, and the result will be stunning in two hours, instead of the fatigue resulting from the eight working hours. In a concert performance, if you don't concentrate one hundred percent and involve your whole being (emotions, will, attention, hearing, and so on), even at the highest level of preparation, it is possible to lose what you have on stage. A professional does not bypass a single detail. To him there are no insignificant notations or instructions in the author's notes. Each stroke is important, and in order to do everything as written, requires a high level of concentration. This is what separates the masters from the amateur".

As you can see, the ability to work at a high level of concentration allows the musician to move from the rank of an 'Amateur' to that of a 'Professional'. And this is true for every skill in life. Only by concentrating can you get far ahead in any business and prosper, leaving your competitors behind. Isn't it a significant advantage having to constantly be in the HERE AND NOW? Dear reader, would you not want to have the same degree of efficiency and effectiveness in your life? Without false modesty, I can say that it is only by using this system of effective concentration in the HERE AND NOW, that I have been able to achieve better results than people who work a lot, but are constantly distracted.

People who can be IN THE HERE AND NOW can:
1. Join the top 3% who controls the world
2. Achieve the level of individuals like: Bill Gates, Yulia Tymoshenko, Margaret Thatcher
3. Achieve outstanding results in any field

The 3% are the people who rule this world, creating a working system that is forced to grow and change the world. These are the people who create jobs and employ, as the serving work-force, the remaining 97% of the people whose consciousness is 'asleep' or non-functional. The 97% set of people have not awakened from their sleep to live — they are sleeping while awake. They usually live on the level of instincts and reactions to external stimuli and neither have their own goals, nor the more specific ways to achieve them. This wise saying warns about such a state: "IF YOU HAVE NO GOALS IN LIFE, YOU HAVE TO WORK FOR THOSE WHO HAVE".

The person who has goals lives in the HERE AND NOW — he or she is 'awake', alert and has an awareness of every moment. Those compelled to work for the man who has goals are people who have their heads in the clouds, sleep-walking or are in fruitless dreams without any implementation. The first names on everyone's lips are people in the 3% category. Such people are either idolized or greatly hated. They are the ones that undertake daring projects and sometimes suffer crushing defeats, but they also know the taste of victory, winners that rise to the top, being not enslaved by the 97% of the population. On the other hand, nobody knows the names of the 97% category of people — they are just a statistic, people whose existence will be forgotten as soon as they leave the earth. They leave this earth, not even leaving a small footprint — nothing to show that they were ever here. These 97% of the population work in the systems which are created by the 3%. In which category of people do you want to be, dear reader?

THE ABILITY TO BE IN THE HERE AND NOW IS POSSIBLE FOR ALL!

Dear reader, with full confidence I say that EVERY MAN IS ABLE TO BE FOCUSED! For certain each of you has sometime been at an interesting movie theatre or participated in a fascinating show. You remember how breath-taking the movie was to you while you were watching — then you were 100% HERE AND NOW. Your vision and hearing perceived everything that was happening on the screen or on the stage, you were absorbed and completely captured by the unfolding events. You enjoyed it! What's more, you often desire to be taken away from your present reality and gladly surrender yourself into the hands of the film producers.

The whole industry is working to entertain you, to help you to be carried away into another reality. It works on all the expensive special effects, thousands of professionals working day and night to make the show exciting so that you could not get away even for a moment. No wonder Hollywood is called the 'dream factory' – this reflects much more accurately the true essence of the film industry. Thus, when watching a good movie, one is in the state of HERE AND NOW but this is an 'artificial concentration' involving external factors such as sound and image.

But there is also the **true concentration** — when a person, by an effort of their own will, is able to keep their presence HERE AND NOW, directing their attention to the selected object. As an example of this true concentration, I would like to give a terrific biography of a deaf-blind American woman, who is the first in the world among people with similar disabilities, to receive higher education, became the author of seven books and was an active public figure.

Helen Adams Keller (1880–1968) was born a perfectly healthy girl. But after a severe illness that lasted a year and a half, she became blind and deaf. Due to this event, the girl soon became uncontrollable, and the parents seriously thought about how to place her in a special institution. But the improbable combination of circumstances helped to avoid this fate to the girl.

From a travelogue the "American Notes" by Charles Dickens, Helen's mother learned about the successes which have been achieved by teachers in the rehabilitation of one deaf-blind girl Laura Bridgman. Helen and her father drove to Baltimore to see a specialist, who after the examination recommended that the family consult Alexander Graham Bell — the inventor of the telephone. Mr. Bell, was also suffering from impaired hearing, and later was completely deaf; and so he devoted his entire life to helping deaf children.

On the suggestion of Mr. Bell, Helen's parents met with the Director of Perkins Institute for the Blind and Helen was given a nurse by the names of Ann Sullivan.

As a child, this lady Ann Sullivan, got ill too and almost lost her sight and was brought up in a shelter for the poor. Despite the illness, she was educated and became a teacher. Anne Sullivan had a decisive influence on the development of Helen Keller, their friendship lasted forty-nine years. Up to seven years, Helen lived almost without any contact with the outside world or nature, so the main task of the new nanny was to establish a good relationship with Helen and restore the confidence of the girl. Anne began to teach Helen the tactile alphabet, drawing on her palm and finger spelling. Helen learned fairly quickly, but there was a challenge — she could not connect the words she learned with the physical objects.

In April, 1887, a miracle happened, which formed the basis of William Gibson's play and the movie — 'The Miracle Worker'. Following an experience at a water pump, Helen understood the word 'w-a-t-e-r' and finally connected it to the 'object'. Within the next few hours she leant thirty words. We can assume that on this day Helen was 'born again', but not in the normal world consisting of colors and sounds, but in the world of letters and words, which brought about fullness of life for her. The thirst for knowledge drove Helen to learn how to read books for the blind and to use a typewriter to express her thoughts. She also learned how to ride a pony and to swim.

From childhood, Helen began to write letters, which aptly revealed the intellectual and spiritual evolution of her personality. By her eighteenth birthday, Helen had mastered Latin, Greek, French and German. Through touch-lip reading, she understood the language of her companions and the fact that words gradually took on material forms was acknowledged by Helen herself.

In 1888, Helen began to work at the Perkins School for the Blind and in 1894, together with Ann, moved to New York where she began to attend Wright-Humason school for the Deaf. In 1898, they both returned to Massachusetts and Helen attended the Cambridge School for Young Ladies, a preparatory school for women. In 1900 she gained admission to Radcliffe College, one of the most prestigious educational institutions at the time. At the request of Mark Twain, Henry Rogers and his wife sponsored Helen's studies and in addition, they supported her with a monthly stipend for many years.

In 1904, at the age of 24 Keller graduated from Radcliffe College with honors and so became the first deaf-blind person to have received a higher education. In 1964, US President Lyndon Johnson awarded her one of the two highest civilian awards in America — The Presidential Medal of Freedom. When Helen Keller died on the eve of her 88th birthday, the memorial service in her honor was held at the Washington National Cathedral, where still rests the urn containing her ashes.

Perhaps you will agree that the lot that fell on Helen Keller was of unimaginable complexity. To us, it would seem that fate has destined her to spend the rest of her life in extreme disability — not having any hearing, eyesight or speech. Despite all this, Helen acquired a unique ability to affect others with a thirst for life and creativity. Even celebrities such as Mark Twain were touched. Through

Helen, it was demonstrated that a person who is practically and completely cut off from the normal world can actually concentrate their efforts and attention to learn and master letters, get a higher education and become the author of numerous books. In my opinion, this is an outstanding example of true concentration. So if this lady managed to do this, then I can say with confidence that the ability to be IN THE HERE AND NOW is available to all!

In conclusion, I want to introduce you to the statements of Helen Keller, which clearly demonstrate what anyone can achieve by the power of their will and attention being directed at a chosen subject:

1. *Even if my vital spark should be blown out, I believe that I should behave with courageous dignity in the presence of fate, and strive to be a worthy companion of the beautiful, the good and the true. But fate has its master in the faith of those who surmount it, and limitation has its limits for those who, though disillusioned, live greatly. True faith is not a fruit of well-being, it is the ability to combine mortal fragility with the inner strength of the spirit. It does not fluctuate after the changing shadows of thought. When I think of the suffering and famine, and the continued slaughter of men, my spirit bleeds. But the thought comes to me that, like the little deaf, dumb and blind child I once was, mankind is growing out of the darkness of ignorance and hate into the light of a brighter day.*

2. *Life is an exciting adventure and the most beautiful life is a life lived for others.*

3. *Many persons have a wrong idea of what constitutes true happiness. It is not attained through self-gratification but through fidelity to a worthy purpose.*

4. *The best and most beautiful things in the world cannot be seen or even touched — they must be felt with the heart.*

5. *Security is mostly a superstition. It does not exist in nature, nor do the children of men as a whole experience it. Avoiding danger is no safer in the long run than outright exposure. Life is either a daring adventure, or nothing.*

6. *No pessimist ever discovered the secret of the stars, or sailed to unchartered land, or opened a new doorway for the human spirit.*

7. *When one door of happiness closes, another opens; but often we look so long at the closed door that we do not see the one which has been opened for us.*

8. *Although the world is full of suffering, it is also full of the overcoming of it.*

9. *To create a society in which everyone cares about the common good is impossible, as long as we will not give up the habit of taking and giving nothing in return.*

10. *The world is moved along, not only by the mighty shoves of its heroes, but also by the aggregate of tiny pushes of each honest worker.*

11. *My share of the work may be limited, but the fact that it is work makes it precious.*

12. *True mercy is the desire to bring benefit to people, without thinking of remuneration.*

13. *Science may have found a cure for most evils; but it has found no remedy for the worst of them all — the apathy of human beings.*

14. *The best educated person is the one who understands life and the circumstances in which he lives.*

15. *We have a lot of courage in general, but very little when it comes to particulars.*

So, dear reader, in this Chapter we talked about what it means to be IN THE HERE AND NOW, about the advantages that the person in this state has, and that EACH person can master this ability — it is not complicated at all! Because it is not as difficult as it might seem at first sight, I want to encourage you, dear reader to LET the HERE AND NOW become your REALITY and your GOAL!

In the next Chapter, we will look at how to be 100% HERE AND NOW — every minute and second of your life. I will share with you, from a practical perspective, what may prevent you from being IN THE HERE AND NOW and the implications.

GOLDEN NUGGETS

1. HERE AND NOW is a state of consciousness in which all attention is focused on what is happening in a place and at that moment.

2. To be IN THE HERE AND NOW, you must engage with what is happening or can happen now, not burdening yourself with the problems of the future.

3. When we manage to focus and direct our thoughts in one direction and on one task, we increase our speed and efficiency of performance ten times over.

4. People who are capable of being IN THE HERE AND NOW enter into the 3 percent of the human population that govern the world — they attain the level of personalities like Bill Gates, Yulia Tymoshenko, Margaret Thatcher and achieve outstanding results in any field of endeavour.

5. The ability to be IN THE HERE AND NOW is available to all!

6. True concentration is when the man himself, by the effort of his own will, keeps his presence HERE AND NOW, directing all his attention on the chosen object, objective or goal.

SELF ASSESSMENT TEST

1. **Can you rec7ite from memory a poem you were taught as a child?**

   a) Yes (2)

   b) No (1)

2. **Can you remember what you ate for breakfast three days ago?**

   a) Yes (2)

   b) No (1)

3. **Do you often relive again what happened in the past?**

   a) Yes (2)

   b) No (1)

Self-assessment test rresults

3 points

Sorry, but your level of concentration is very low. This suggests that you are rarely HERE AND NOW. You find it hard to focus and direct your thoughts in the direction that you need at that particular moment. But don't despair! You have already discovered that the ability to be IN THE HERE AND NOW is available to all. Make the effort to work on yourself and you can expect different results. This book you are holding in your hands will help you.

4–5 points

Not Bad! With varying degrees of success, you manage to be IN THE HERE AND NOW. Sometimes you lose control of your thoughts, and they can carry you into the past or future, denying the sense of reality of what is happening. You are encouraged to develop your level of concentration, for which I advise you to read the remaining chapters of this book, paying special attention to the practical exercises at the end of each chapter.

6 points

Excellent! Most of the time you can be IN THE HERE AND NOW, not wasting time on fruitless experiences of the past or groundless fantasies about the future. You're able to concentrate your thoughts to help you achieve success in life. You have learned a lot. I advise you to share your experiences with the people around you.

RECOMMENDATIONS ON CARRYING OUT THE PRACTICAL TASKS

1. ATTENTION! The practical tasks listed after each Chapter are not just for reading; you need them. With my years of experience with people, I know that oftentimes, people perform these tasks just 'to tick the box', as if in school; but this is your life, this is for you, take the assignments seriously.

2. For maximum results we recommend you perform the tasks within 24 hours, otherwise, leaving them for later, you are distancing yourself from your destiny and your success.

3. To answer all the questions, work out the practical tasks in a serene and tranquil environment. Find a quiet place where no one will be able to interfere; perhaps a time when no one is at home; or at night when everyone is asleep.

4. Be sure to reflect on the previous Chapter and go over all the items which you emphasized for yourself. Remember the decisions you made and write down your subsequent actions.

5. Certainly put specific time deadlines planned, and define restrictions which you will apply in relation to yourself; it will help you not to shelve implementation of the decisions you made.

6. Find someone to whom you could be accountable regarding your decisions, who could remind you of them — a kind of partner in working on yourself.

PRACTICAL TASKS

1. How do you understand what it means to be IN THE HERE AND NOW? Suggest five definitions.

2. What advantages do you see in constantly being HERE AND NOW? Itemize the benefits that you are going to enjoy.

3. What example of true concentration can you see by the example of Helen Keller, the deaf-blind American who was the first among such people to receive higher education, and has authored seven books? What conclusions can you make for yourself from that exemplary story?

4. To develop your awareness and to increase the time when you are in a conscious state, here is a useful technique you can apply: Place a rubber band around your wrist, and every time you catch yourself having lost the awareness of this wrist band, snap the rubber band. This shows that you had ceased to be IN THE HERE AND NOW — you had forgotten about the rubber band, your thoughts had wandered off into the past or future. The mild pain that the rubber band gives acts as a wake-up call back to the present moment.

5. It would also be useful to ask yourself these sobering questions: "Am I asleep now or not?" "Am I awake or not?" Such thoughts help create a new and completely different outlook on life.

CHAPTER 6

HOW TO BE 100% IN THE HERE AND NOW

For many years I have studied success and found a lot of useful rules. But it is absolutely necessary to observe only one — the principle of full concentration. If you can devote all your attention and energy to a task, clearly understand what the task is all about and focus only on it until it is completed, you will be able to conquer the world. You will be able to achieve any goal, overcome any obstacle, become rich, successful, happy and live a long life.

BRIAN TRACY

As you probably will remember, dear reader, that in the previous Chapter we looked at what it means to be IN THE HERE AND NOW, and the advantage of this ability or skill. You also learned that everyone has the ability to be IN THE HERE AND NOW. Therefore I hope that you too will join those for whom being IN THE HERE AND NOW is an unshakable reality of every moment, every second. According to Brian Tracy, being 100% HERE AND NOW is the principle of "full concentration"; and its application "conquers the world, achieves any goal, overcomes any obstacle", and enables one "to become rich, successful, happy and to live a long life." Isn't this the dream of almost every person on earth? Let's look at how we can apply this principle in our lives and how to achieve what we want. We can start with familiarizing ourselves with very important statements.

THREE TYPES OF PRESENCE

There are three types of presence:
1) Physical (only the 'body')
2) Selective (irregular)
3) HERE AND NOW — the mind of such a person is always fully engaged and each of his step is consciously taken.

Let us consider in more detail each of these types.

So, the **first type of presence** is when a person may be physically present; they may be looking at you and you know that they are right in front of you, but actually they are not there; it's only the body that is present there with you as an inanimate object. His whole appearance says "My body is with you," but the truth is that he is 'lost' in his thoughts. It is the case that we considered when Antonina Petrovna's thoughts flew to her mother in the country, while only her body was present at the workshop.

The **second type of presence** is when a person is present selectively; they selectively join in the subject line only if it is interesting to them.

Catherine was one of the best students at the University. And now, sitting on a chair, she continued enthusiastically to work on the computer, having half an ear on what was happening in the classroom. This was the seminar in which, according to the advice of their teacher, the students put 'their two cents'. There were some smart Professors whom Catherine believed in. As soon as these teachers took the floor, she would drop everything and listen very intently. Nikolai Nikolaevich was one of such teachers and knew how to captivatingly talk about his subject, so that he could capture and hold student's attention. Often the students came from other departments to his lectures because they were so interesting. What can I say, it was evident that Nikolai invested his heart and soul into his work!

But that day, not only was it about listening to the famous Nikolai Nikolaevich, to a bunch of opinions from some 'narrow-minded' students as well. Catherine smiled and comforted herself, "It's okay, when one of them takes the floor, I will switch to my business." As a single-minded girl, she preferred not to waste time and was quite sure that listening to 'nonsense' was absolutely a waste of time. In fact, she did not see anything wrong in 'shutting down' while one of those 'losers', according to Catherine, was speaking. It was okay to be unsympathetic and ignore what they had to say.

Unfortunately, Catherine is not the only one in our society that thinks like this.

If we consider what someone else says as unimportant, it only shows that we have no culture of respect for others.

Respect for people suggests that we listen carefully to them when they speak. What we think about others — "He can't say anything sensible" or "She always talks a lot and still nothing", these are just our prejudices against those people. First, we mentally decide that we should not expect anything good from this person; then we carefully seek and find confirmation to these expectations and then automatically 'switch off' as soon as they start to speak because we have certainty decided what the result will be in advance. At the end of the day, we miss out on what this person could have enriched our lives with, because each of us, with rare exceptions, is in a constant process of development and improvement. And the fact that this person could not say anything sensible before, nor construct a perfect sentence, does not automatically mean that they will face the same failure in the future.

EACH PERSON SHOULD ALWAYS LISTEN VERY ATTENTIVELY, WITHOUT SWITCHING OFF NOR ENGAGING IN PARALLEL THINKING. It will be easy to do, when we understand and realize the value of every person and their uniqueness; when we begin to understand that, not only within ourselves but also to express the respect for others by listening to them.

Selective (irregular) hearing or a selective presence in the HERE AND NOW shows how human beings are by nature self-centered and tend to be selfish in the way we choose those who we want to associate with — "*If a person can prove useful to me, then I will listen to them, if not, I will switch off*". This suggests that our motives are self-centered and we seek only to meet our own needs. We do not have nor show interest in other people, we tend to ignore people as if they were invisible. By so doing, we are destroying each other and multiplying the level of indifference in this world. Thus, we do not bring into this world even a little bit of good, we do not make it purer and better.

The **third type of presence** is when the person is HERE AND NOW. This final level of presence allows a person to learn on the fly, such people are capable of extracting 'tiny pearls'. I want to tell you, dear reader, that we must practice only this kind of presence in our lives.

I often get asked how I manage to remember people — their faces and names. For all of my life, there is a large number of people I have met and it seems so incredible that it is possible for me to remember almost everyone of them. It does not matter the many years after our first meeting, I am able to recognize someone — I say "Hello", remember their name and even what we talked about. But I don't see anything extraordinary about this. The explanation is simple — this exceptional memory lies in the fact that I am always HERE AND NOW. I never 'roll' into another reality, I'm never carried away by thoughts to some other place. When I talk to people, I am 100% focused on the conversation with them. It allows me to remember the details effortlessly. If you are 100% HERE AND NOW whenever you communicate with someone, you don't even need to exert yourself to keep in memory the details of the meeting, the face of a person, their name or the essence of the conversation.

People say to me: *"It's amazing that you are never confused"*, *"You never lose your focus"* or *"You always have something to say or add!"* Yes, exactly! I never get lost, and I always have something to say. This is all because I continuously put my brain to work — am always HERE AND NOW because I take every step consciously.

WHAT CAN PREVENT YOU FROM BEING IN THE HERE AND NOW

On our path to full concentration, to ensure that we are 100% HERE AND NOW, there are behaviours that can hinder us. Therefore I suggest that you, dear reader, should identify them and learn how to deal with them.

Now, the following can prevent you from being HERE AND NOW:

- Parallel thinking
- Multi-tasking
- Inability to see the value of another person
- Introversion

PARALLEL THINKING

The golden rule of communication states: **At the time when you listen, AVOID YOU CANNOT THINK IN PARALLEL, otherwise you won't hear the other party!**

To think in parallel means to 'be on the wave' and not to be IN THE HERE AND NOW. Maybe you are familiar with a situation whereby people seem to be listening to you, but are actually thinking about their response — *"And what can I say in response?" "How do I cut him short?" "I really want to talk about my grievance", "How do I look? I wonder what he thinks of me?" "Behold the man (woman)!"* When you are HERE AND NOW, it is impossible to think in parallel while the other person is speaking. This is strictly forbidden!

For this reason, any communication or conversation with such a person is unproductive since they are mentally busy with what they want to say. As a matter of fact, this person is not listening but only politely (and sometimes not very) waiting for their turn to speak and make an impression. If no one listens, then there will be no dialogue but monologues of two people who have met, said what they wanted and left without exchanging views. Each of them will only remember just what he said and not the words of the other party. Is this being 100% HERE AND NOW?

THE DESIRE TO MULTI-TASK

In today's world, all processes are constantly accelerating. Everything is done much faster, we are constantly searching for ways to perform the same tasks with minimal time and effort. To save time, people have thought to combine many of the processes, to do several things at the same time. It must be admitted that in many cases this is straightforward, but not always. To carry out multiple tasks at the same time is only possible where the special attention of the person is not required, and there are no negative consequences using a specific device to perform the task automatically. However, there are times when this cannot be done, and there is need to focus on the case that requires our full concentration on what is happening — it is necessary to be 100% HERE AND NOW.

THE INABILITY TO SEE THE VALUE OF ANOTHER PERSON

Alexei Maximovich Gorky, Russian writer, novelist, playwright, said, *"Each person has a hidden bell and when affected, sounds it the best he can."* Isn't that an interesting statement? These words mean that no matter how similar we may look by outward appearance, the most important aspects of each person are hidden within them. This invisible treasure is sometimes imperceptible to the naked eye, but when under a conducive environment, it may be disclosed and enabled to fill the world around with wonderful and unique music. The 'bell' is the value and uniqueness you need to learn to appreciate and respect whenever we meet anyone.

In this regard, there is one very interesting study.

Researchers asked for the help of a group of school teachers. These teachers were told that the choice fell on them due to their exceptional teaching abilities. In addition, they were told that their classes would consist of only gifted children, but neither the children nor their parents would know anything about the experiment, because the goal was to find out how these gifted children could behave if they were not aware of their abilities.

As expected, in the teachers' reports, they wrote that the children managed exceptionally well. In addition, they wrote that working with these children was a pleasure and that they would like to carry on working with them.

However, this project had one secret appendix — the teachers did not know that they were not selected based on any exceptional abilities but was done arbitrarily. And that the children were not selected on the basis of giftedness but randomly. So, since the expectations were high, the results were high. Both the teachers and the children believed in themselves as exceptional and therefore were able to achieve exceptional success.

What does this mean for us? Our **preconceptions (expectations)**, previously formed on the basis of any information, have a huge impact on how we listen to people and what we will eventually hear. If we get rid of our biases or try to minimize them, then we can learn to really listen and hear those around us. **But our prejudices can play a dirty trick on us:** IF WE 'WRITE OFF' SOMEONE, WE CAN NEVER FIND ANYTHING OF VALUE IN WHAT THEY HAVE TO SAY. When we pay attention to people as though their words contain something important and precious, then we find that 'hidden treasure'.

SELF-FOCUS

Because people most often focus on themselves and think only about themselves, they are constantly living in fear and anxiety about their appearance or ability to speak to an audience. Focussing on one's personal appearance can prevent a person from being a good listener or speaker in order to perceive the information HERE AND NOW and then to be effective in achieving the results.

This problem is especially common for ladies. When you go to make a public speech, forget about your gender or that person you want to impress. At this point, there is no time to be thinking about how well-fitting your skirt is or worrying about the neckline and the hairdo. You have had time at home, in front of the mirror, to fix all these. You should never wear uncomfortable clothing because when you are not confident of your appearance — carrying out on-the-spot checks and always having something to adjust during the talk, then you cease to be IN THE HERE AND NOW. You are unable to convey the message to the audience thereby destroying the first and last impression that you came to make. That is why many women in the West are more casual in their dressing; wearing only what is convenient and comfortable. This way, one has nothing to worry about.

To be fully HERE AND NOW that is 100%, it is necessary to get rid of focussing on ourselves. Whether speaking or listening, one has to put one's ego aside as much as possible by shifting the focus from oneself during the whole communication process. Think about, primarily, what the other person is saying or about what message you need to convey to the audience. At any given moment, the 'I' must not be at the start of the communication process.

HOW TO LISTEN OR SPEAK IN THE 'HERE AND NOW' STATE

Even with listening, it is necessary to be IN THE HERE AND NOW. Without the ability to listen with 100% attention, it is impossible to be IN THE HERE AND NOW. We have to concentrate on listening first; connecting all of our senses of perception, sight, hearing to receive the information given. It is only after we have concentrated on taking in the information given us that we can begin to process it HERE AND NOW.

As we have said in the first Chapter of this book, the reason for problems such as forgetfulness, absent mindedness, lack of or low level of perseverance, is that people do not penetrate into the essence of conversation. To avoid such failures in the perception of information, it is NECESSARY to CONNECT ALL senses to HEAR AND LISTEN at 100%.

How to listen in the HERE AND NOW state
- Every cell of your being must work only on your absorption in the communication process
- Everything else ceases to exist at this point, not even your name!
- You must not think about what you want to say in response

How to speak in the HERE AND NOW state
- There must be only one thought — the one that you want to convey
- Everything else must cease to exist for you

There can be only two states:

1. you are either speaking

2. or you are listening and taking in information

How to help yourself achieve the state of listening HERE AND NOW

Your posture should show a readiness to listen and learn;

- Look at the mouth of the speaker
- Sit on the edge of your seat
- Do not cross the legs
- Sit upright not reclined

Test: *Try to repeat what the speaker said a few minutes ago.*

So, in this Chapter we have seen how to be 100% HERE AND NOW. You have learned about the three types of presence and identified the hindrances to being HERE AND NOW. You have also learned how to listen and speak, in the HERE AND NOW state. In the next Chapter, we shall talk about what will help us to be IN THE HERE AND NOW.

GOLDEN NUGGETS

1. There are three types of presence:

   a. Physical

   b. Selective

   c. HERE AND NOW

2. Each person should always listen very attentively without switching off nor trying to think in parallel

3. If the person is HERE AND NOW, it allows him to learn 'on the fly' and to retrieve pearls from the seemingly insignificant people.

4. When you listen, avoid PARALLEL THINKING, otherwise you won't hear the conversation!

5. To be IN THE HERE AND NOW, you cannot be multi-tasking

6. To be IN THE HERE AND NOW, you need to avoid focusing on yourself

7. In order to avoid failures in the perception of any information, it is necessary to connect all your senses to listen and hear 100%

8. There can be only two states: you're either speaking or listening.

SELF-ASSESSMENT

1. **I try to end the conversation as quickly as possible, if I am not interested in the topic nor the speaker.**

   a) Almost always (0)
   b) As a general rule (1)
   c) Occasionally (3)
   d) It is very rare (4)

2. **I often interrupt others while they are speaking.**

   a) Almost always (0)
   b) As a general rule (1)
   c) Occasionally (3)
   d) It is very rare (4)

3. **During conversations, I often pretend to listen, but in reality I think about myself.**

   a) Almost always (0)
   b) As a rule (1)
   c) Sometimes (3)
   d) Very seldom (4)

Self-assessment results

0–3 points

Sorry, but about how to be IN THE HERE AND NOW, you can only dream of it. Obviously, you need to learn to listen during conversations and not to get distracted. Stop thinking about your own affairs in the middle of a communication process. You need to learn how to practice the third kind of presence. The exercise described in the last chapter of the book will help you.

4–8 points

Your effort to be IN THE HERE AND NOW is commendable but apparently, you do not always succeed. You still have the habit of parallel thinking while the other person is talking and you are still driven by the desire to multi-task. The exercise at the end of the book will help you to get rid of that which prevents you from being HERE AND NOW. We wish you success in mastering new techniques!

9–12 points

Congratulations! You have successfully overcome all that prevents you from being IN THE HERE AND NOW every second of your life. Out of the three types of presence, practice the third most often in your life. It helps you to give 100% attention to listening and hearing when somebody is talking. This can only give rise to respect and admiration. Continue to remain the best, and help others to become like you!

RECOMMENDATIONS
ON CARRYING OUT THE
PRACTICAL TASKS

1. ATTENTION! The practical tasks listed after each Chapter are not just for reading; you need them. With my years of experience with people, I know that oftentimes, people perform these tasks just 'to tick the box', as if in school; but this is your life, this is for you, take the assignments seriously.

2. For maximum results we recommend you perform the tasks within 24 hours, otherwise, leaving them for later, you are distancing yourself from your destiny and your success.

3. To answer all the questions, work out the practical tasks in a serene and tranquil environment. Find a quiet place where no one will be able to interfere; perhaps a time when no one is at home; or at night when everyone is asleep.

4. Be sure to reflect on the previous Chapter and go over all the items which you emphasized for yourself. Remember the decisions you made and write down your subsequent actions.

5. Certainly put specific time deadlines planned, and define restrictions which you will apply in relation to yourself; it will help you not to shelve implementation of the decisions you made.

6. Find someone to whom you could be accountable regarding your decisions, who could remind you of them — a kind of partner in working on yourself.

PRACTICAL TASKS

1. Based on the points above, examine yourself —
   How often are you able to be IN THE HERE AND
   NOW? In which of the three modes of presence
   are you more often? Work out for yourself the
   steps that will allow you to increase the percentage
   of your presence in the HERE AND NOW.

2. What is the Golden rule of communication?
   How often have you ignored this principle,
   and what has been the result? How do
   you intend to apply the Golden rule of
   communication in your life from now on?

3. What prevents people from being HERE AND
   NOW? For each reason, explain why it is undesirable.

CHAPTER 7

WHAT CAN HELP TO BE IN THE HERE AND NOW

WHAT CAN HELP TO BE IN THE HERE AND NOW

In the previous chapter we looked at how to be 100% HERE AND NOW. You now know, dear reader, that there are three types of presence and can identify the hindrances to being HERE AND NOW. You have also learned how to listen and speak in the HERE AND NOW state. In this chapter, you will learn how to stop 'soaring in the clouds', which will help you remain HERE AND NOW every minute, every second of your life. It is absolutely necessary for us to master this skill.

STAY FOCUSED

Concentration is the secret of strength in politics, in war, in trade, in short, in all management of human affairs.
RALPH WALDO EMERSON

To be in the HERE AND NOW, you need to maintain consistency and focus of your thoughts. Isaac Newton (1642–1727), English physicist, mathematician, engineer and astronomer, one of the founders of classical physics, made this definition: *"Genius is the patience of thoughts, concentrated in a certain direction"*. According to a Brief Psycho-Philological Dictionary by A.V. Filippov, N.N. Romanova and T.V. Letyagovy, *"**concentration** is the state of the individual when his attention and thoughts focus on one subject long enough without unintentionally diverting to other objects."* Synonyms of the word 'focus' include: seriousness, determination, concentration, direction, recording, collection, fixity, thoughtfully, thoroughness, attentiveness, care.

Genuine concentration is a condition in which the mind is focused and thus acquires power and energy. Imagine how a convex lens works. The rays of sunlight falling on a piece of paper can only make it warm because the rays are parallel to each other. But if the same beam of light passed through a convex lens, the paper would ignite! This is because the lens causes the rays to converge to a focal point and the effect of this becomes enormous! In the same way, concentration becomes that same 'lens' that increases the flow of our mental energy, allowing us to achieve outstanding results.

All the great men whose names are well known: Mikhailo Lomonosov, Dmitri Mendeleev, Albert Einstein, Thomas Edison, Isaac Newton and many others, focused on the study of some particular subject. That is why they were able to make scientific discoveries, thus providing scientific and technological progress and moving humanity forward in development. The words of Ralph Waldo Emerson (1803–1882) American essayist, poet, philosopher, pastor, social activist; one of the most prominent thinkers and writers of the USA, which I used as an epigraph to this Chapter suggests the same: "Concentration *is the secret of strength in politics, in war, in trade, in short, in all management of human affairs.*" Concentration can be on any subject of conversation, discussion, meditation, and so on. Concentration leads to a breakthrough — a qualitative leap, the transition to a new level of knowledge, skills, and achievements. Herein lies, in fact, the nature of genius.

Why do most people live as a 'grey mass' - living unconsciously? This is because they don't bother to **focus their thoughts.** When a person does not want to take the trouble to engage his mind, his thoughts are chaotic and point in different directions; he suffers a predictable failure. Disorganized thoughts carry the owner either into the experiences of the past, or into the impossible dreams of the future, not allowing him to focus on what is happening HERE AND NOW. It's like a man trying to strike a blow, not with a fist, but with the fingers spread out, won't get any success but only hurt fingers. You get similar results trying to achieve something significant in life, but not concentrating your thoughts and organizing your thinking process. All such attempts will fail!

So, in order to be IN THE HERE AND NOW, you need to:
1. **Decide**

2. **Select the object of focus, concentration** —
    a comprehensive, all-consuming goal: if the goal is not essential to the man, it is hard to be self-disciplined.

3. **Maintain consistency and focus thoughts** — concentration of thought

If you have no goals in life or don't live for something specific in order to get a certain result, then you will find it hard to maintain this continuity of thought. The thoughts of a man should be focussed only on his goal. Either we live for a purpose, consciously achieving it — that is, doing everything possible to see the solution of this task, and for this, overcome obstacles, go through some deprivations and restrictions on its part; or we simply laze around in life, or as you read above, live the life of a 'grey mass' or 'bio-mass' - when people live unconsciously and do not bother to engage their minds all through their years on earth.

BLOCK ALL DISTRACTIONS

We must keep our minds immune to distractions. If a man's eyes are drawn to a subject, but his mind is being pulled away by the cares of the world, he can't focus on the knowledge of the truth.
SAINT BASIL THE GREAT

Sergei dreamed of becoming a writer of international renown. He had long wanted to finish writing the book that would become a product of the creative process, which lasted for that year. Of course, he would like to see this work become a masterpiece and make a splash

beyond the literary world. He already envisioned a book just published with many thousands copies of having his name on the cover pages, and the crowd wanting to buy the new book by Sergei Malevsky lining up in front of the bookstore early in the morning to make the long-awaited purchase. In this mind, he could see the faces of the fans, surging around him asking for autographs!

All these pictures were painted in the imagination of Sergei. He sat in front of a sheet of blank paper; he was holding a pen in his hands with the intent to write the next chapter. But wait! He forgot the most important thing: it is urgent to discuss plans for next summer with his wife today, they have not been on vacation, and he had to think carefully about the trip to the sea. By the way, it would be nice to find out from his wife's opinion about the next political crisis in the country. In addition, Sergei got yet another call from work and was informed that the next project deadlines had shifted: all the necessary reports ought to be handed over a week earlier. "Oh no! Working on the next chapter today is just impossible. Perhaps, I will return to it tomorrow when there are less cares," thought Sergei as he put down the pen. The sheet of paper remained untouched. Grabbing a bag of documents, Sergei fled to solve operational issues, answering a phone call on the way.

The work on the book continued for years, but there is no need to talk about the completion of what was, he had started...

It is so sad that Sergei didn't manage to cope with flow of the urgent and important issues capturing his daily life. In fact, he had to postpone the execution of the mission again indefinitely. He didn't manage to cope with those hindrances which inevitably arise in the life of every human being that gets ready to carry out any intention. The verdict is inevitable — if a person decides to write a book and during the time allotted for this, begins to think about his wife, about the office, about the problems of society, he will not succeed! When a person sits at his desk with the intention to complete the next Chapter of his book, this is not the time to address all other issues. All other thoughts at that moment are a hindrance to the implementation of the plan, one needs to BLOCK them out!

In our lives there can be countless hindrances and obstacles as we move towards our goal. Why do you think celebrities don't poke their nose into the street; and even if they appear in public places, they try to hide or change their appearance so that no one would recognize them? If a public figure without an armed escort, ventures out into the street, he or she is unlikely to get to their destination. Along the way they will meet a lot of people, each of whom will want to ask a question, or get an autograph, or, God forbid, express their discontent by picking up a fight. In addition, there are many mentally ill people, who for the sake of themselves becoming famous, would dare to injure or even kill a celebrity, as was the case with John Lennon.

Therefore the guard, whose task is to ensure the safe arrival of a celebrity to their destination, does everything possible to block any interference that the VIP may encounter. This will ensure uninterrupted passage of the protected persons to their planned destination. And it's not so much a thing of pride on the part of a public figure to go with security, as it may seem at first sight; it is a necessity of life. Otherwise, only few known people go without an escort and refrain from responding to on-lookers, 'entertaining' them by answering their questions or just giving them attention. If you want to look like a democratic person, who is accessible to people at any time of the day or night, this may be beneficial to you. But then you will have to forget the goal, because there will be too many things invading and interfering in your life without your knowledge and keeping you quite busy with many other things.

So, to stop soaring in the clouds and be right here, right now, you need to:

1. Block out of your life and thoughts **any moments** that distract from the goal or theme

   that you have set yourself to work (even if these are good thoughts).

2. Isolate your thoughts from all other directions — that is, **forbid yourself to think outside the goal**, forbid thinking or being engaged in whatever takes you aside from the plan.

At the beginning of this sub-chapter in the epigraph are the words of Basil the Great (330–379), Archbishop of Caesarea in Cappadocia, religious writer and theologian who argued that *"we must keep our minds immune to interference"*. This means that we must learn to block out all distractions that prevent us from being HERE AND NOW, to be able to isolate ourselves from everything that at the given moment doesn't correspond to the purpose of our reasoning, words or actions.

USE THE POWER OF INTENTION

*A significant achievement is to voluntarily
set yourself a difficult goal and firmly hold
on to it in your consciousness.*
WILLIAM JAMES, PSYCHOLOGIST

To stop soaring in the clouds, and always and everywhere be 100% HERE AND NOW, you want to use the power of intention:

- *Identify the result you want to get* — clearly define for yourself what fruit, what result you are going to get as a result of your activities.

- *Decide to pursue a goal, to hit the target* — "I want to think about my goal, to achieve the result which I have set for myself. I only think about it!"

The 'Power of Intention' states the following: *"Up until I get what I intend to get, I don't stop, and I don't get distracted — I don't cease to be IN THE HERE AND NOW!"* Anyone who has decided to follow a chosen direction or decision, does not recede nor give up. The words of the English poet, Philip Sydney (1554–1586), are like a rule, *"Either I'll find a way, or I'll invent one."* By the way, the author of these words was the living embodiment of that same principle — at the court of Queen Elizabeth, he not only displayed intelligence, elegant manners and education, but the courage and warlike tastes, the extraordinary love for adventure and risky expeditions as well. At the early age of 32, Philip had fully lived his life.

People applying the power of intention in their lives have determination, that is, a conscious and active orientation to the result of a particular activity. The most important thing is that such a person **knows exactly what he wants, where he will get it, and what he will be fighting against.**

Thanks to dedication, that the American author in the field of new thought, and one of the founders of the modern genre of 'personal-success' — Napoleon Hill (1883–1970), said, *"A strong man will be defeated by a determined child."*

Many people who have achieved success in this world cause not only the envy of others, but also irritation. They are often accused of being crazy[4] — obsessed with the goal, they don't stop until they get it, they charge towards the goal despite any obstacle or opposition that they encounter. But if you think about it, the only annoying factor in their behavior is just the **power of intention**, which is not found in everyone everywhere. When one overcomes inaction and lack of a vision, they simply get results that others may feel uneasy with. And then the people who generally belong to 'grey mass', are tormented by the question: "Who am I against? This upstart?" But it is quite easy to determine their position — the great American romantic writer, often called the 'Father of American Literature' Washington Irving (1783–1859), said, *"Great minds have purpose, others have wishes. Little minds are tamed and subdued by misfortunes; but great minds rise above them."*

Absence of the power of intention leaves a person in a crowd of dreamers — those who sleep in reality, indulging in fruitless dreams and fantasies (and there are so many on

4   Crazy — when a person is capable of reckless, risky behaviour.

this earth). Unfortunately, such people are unable to change anything in this world. This world is changed only by those who set specific goals and stubbornly go after them until they attain them. NOTHING CHANGES IN OUR LIVES UNTIL WE CHANGE. If you continue to do what you have always done — to lose focus, have your mind in the clouds, then you'll continue to have the same result which you have always had. But if you don't like it, and you want to radically change the direction of your life, it is important to make a decision, "*I will always be IN THE HERE AND NOW — listening 100%, reading 100% and reflecting 100%.*" You will learn how to do this practically in the next Chapter.

So I think that this Chapter was not useless to you, dear reader. After reading it, I hope you have understood that it will help you to always and everywhere be IN THE HERE AND NOW. Sure, the practical tips that were given in this Chapter:

1. Learn to be focused
2. Learn to block out distractions
3. Use the power of intention

... will help you realize this in practice.

In the next Chapter, we shall consider the reality that affects what becomes our reality, and how to develop this every day of your life. Stay tuned! Until then, please refer to the Golden nuggets that will remind you of the main ideas explored in Chapter 7 and attempt the test that will help to evaluate your skills. Oh.. and don't forget to carry out the practical tasks!

GOLDEN NUGGETS

1. *"Genius is patience — thoughts that are concentrated in a certain direction"* — Isaac Newton

2. To be IN THE HERE AND NOW, you need to:

   a. Decide

   b. Select the object of focus and concentration

   c. Maintain consistency and focus of thought

3. To stop soaring in the clouds and be IN THE HERE AND NOW, it is necessary to:

   a. Block out from your life or thoughts any moments that distract you from the purpose or theme that you have set yourself to work on (even if it is a good thought)

   b. Isolate your thoughts from all other directions i.e. forbid yourself to think outside the goal, forbid yourself to think or be occupied with distractions.

4. The Power of Intention involves defining the result that the person wishes to receive, as well as the decision to achieve the stated goal.

5. Nothing changes in our lives until we change.

SELF ASSESSMENT

1. **How often do you manage to be focused?**

   a) It is unrealistic! (0)
   b) Rarely (1)
   c) Hard (2)
   d) Always (4)

2. **How do you manage to block out all distractions in your thinking?**

   a) It is unrealistic! (0)
   b) Rarely (1)
   c) Hard (2)
   d) Always (4)

3. **Are you using the Power of Intention to carry out the results that you have defined for yourself?**

   a) No (0)
   b) Rarely (1)
   c) Mostly, Yes (3)
   d) Always (4)

Assessment test results

0–3 points

Sorry, you are rarely able to focus and block out distractions in your thoughts in order to be always in the HERE AND NOW. Therefore you find it is difficult to concentrate and not to 'fly' away in your thoughts to somewhere at every opportunity. To stop soaring in the clouds, you are strongly advised to study the remaining chapter of the book that you now hold in your hands.

4–8 points

Not Bad! You are halfway to permanently overcoming the 'hovering' in the clouds and begin to constantly be in the HERE AND NOW. But at the moment, your level of focus — the ability to get rid of interferences in your thinking and perception leaves much to be desired. You will also need to develop your power of intention, which will allow you to achieve your goals. Carefully studying this book will surely help you to achieve the best results. We wish you all the success!

9–12 points

Congratulations! You passed the test perfectly, which suggests that your level of soaring velocity in the clouds is nil — you almost never do it! Your level of focus and the power of intention to implement your plans almost goes through the roof! Also, you successfully deal with problems that try to divert your attention from the goal. You have the ability to be IN THE HERE AND NOW. Share your skills with others at each and every opportunity!

RECOMMENDATIONS ON CARRYING OUT THE PRACTICAL TASKS

1. ATTENTION! The practical tasks listed after each Chapter are not just for reading; you need them. With my years of experience with people, I know that oftentimes, people perform these tasks just 'to tick the box', as if in school; but this is your life, this is for you, take the assignments seriously.

2. For maximum results we recommend you perform the tasks within 24 hours, otherwise, leaving them for later, you are distancing yourself from your destiny and your success.

3. To answer all the questions, work out the practical tasks in a serene and tranquil environment. Find a quiet place where no one will be able to interfere; perhaps a time when no one is at home; or at night when everyone is asleep.

4. Be sure to reflect on the previous Chapter and go over all the items which you emphasized for yourself. Remember the decisions you made and write down your subsequent actions.

5. Certainly put specific time deadlines planned, and define restrictions which you will apply in relation to yourself; it will help you not to shelve implementation of the decisions you made.

6. Find someone to whom you could be accountable regarding your decisions, who could remind you of them — a kind of partner in working on yourself.

PRACTICAL TASKS

1. Explain what it means to be focussed. Why is it necessary to be focussed? Do you consider yourself to be a focussed person? What are you going to do in order to become more focussed?

2. Explain what the principle of 'blocking distractions' does in order prevent 'your mind from soaring in the clouds'. How are you going to apply it in your life?

3. What does it mean to use the 'power of intention' in order to be IN THE HERE AND NOW? How are you going to apply this principle in your life?

CHAPTER 8

WHAT IS OUR REALITY?

Man is located where his thoughts are located. Therefore try so that your thoughts would be located where YOU WANT to be.

RABBI NACHMAN OF
BRASLAV, XVIII CENTURY

In the previous chapter we found out the following:

- Be focused
- Block distractions
- Use the power of intention

These principles can help us to always and everywhere be IN THE HERE AND NOW. This Chapter is another intriguing one, in which we shall try to understand THE FACTS that affect what becomes our reality and how to cultivate them every day of our lives. Continue reading and you'll learn many other interesting things!

HOW TO SURVIVE IN THE MIDST OF TERRIBLE SITUATIONS

Viktor Frankl (1905–1997), Austrian psychiatrist, psychologist and neurologist, before the Second World

War, was in Nazi concentration camps from 1942 to 1945 and deeply studied the psychology of depression and suicide. Even in this tribulation period, he did not waste any time. From the beginning to the end of his stay in the concentration camps, this now world-renowned psychiatrist and psychologist was devoted to his medical career. Together with other psychiatrists and social workers from all over Central Europe, he continued to provide specialized assistance to fellow prisoners. Victor Frankl joined the medical community, aiming to assist people in inhumane conditions and faced with unbearable challenges beyond their psyche, intellectual and mental state, to overcome the shock and learn how to survive in the midst of an unbearable reality. The doctors tried to help people whose state can be described by the words of one elderly woman, "I slept at night, and suffered in the daytime."

His immersion in the new and very unusual conditions occurred during the transportation of prisoners from the local prison to the camp. And there was a pattern — the shorter the distance, the slower the car moved, because the Nazis needed some time to 'break' the people, to bring them to the level of 'non-humans', to get them to lose their human form. All the way to the camp, people were subjected to almost continuous torture. The nature of torture depended on the imagination of the SS-escorts, although there was a mandatory set: beating with whips, kicks in the face, abdomen and groin, bullet and bayonet wounds. All these acts were interspersed with procedures that caused extreme fatigue of the body — for example, prisoners spend hours kneeling, etc. Shots were heard from time to time, this meant that someone had been shot. It was forbidden to help themselves or each other dress up. The guards also forced prisoners to insult and beat each other, to blaspheme, to vilify their wives and so on. This is just a partial list of the psychological and physical torture prisoners were subjected to. Because not everyone had the strength to endure such inhumane conditions, many either became insane or committed suicide.

Nevertheless, physicians, among whom was Victor Frankl, continued their activities. In addition, they were forced to hide and keep it secret from the SS-escorts. The conditions of their service to prisoners and their very existence, like for all prisoners, were terrible and the chance of survival minimal. The most important thing they did was to offer 'underground' psychological assistance to the group; they tried to prevent suicide. The motto for the entire psychotherapeutic work carried out in the concentration camp were the words of Friedrich Nietzsche (1844–1900), German philosopher and classical philologist, composer, creator of original philosophical doctrine, which is emphatically non-academic in nature and partly because it has a wide distribution beyond the scientific and philosophical community: "He who has a WHY to live for can bear almost any HOW".

Psychiatrists offered prisoners to use the technique of auto-suggestion, which allowed people to mentally leave their current circumstances. Victor himself often used this technique to remove himself from the surrounding suffering. He describes the feelings as follows: "So, I remember one morning going from the camp, unable to endure hunger any longer, the cold and pain in the foot, swollen from dropsy, frostbitten and festering — my situation seemed to be hopeless.

Then I imagined myself standing at the pulpit in a large, beautiful, warm and bright, lecture hall in front of an interested audience, I lectured on the topic 'Group psychotherapeutic experiences in a concentration camp' and talked about everything that I experienced. Believe me, at that moment I never believed that the day would come when I could have the opportunity to deliver such a lecture".

Have you noticed, dear reader, what Victor Frankl practically did in order to keep his sanity — how he did not let his awareness of the negative reality break him? Despite the horrific external conditions, **Frankl focused his attention on what his soul aspired for; what he chose to think of himself.** After going through the hell of the concentration camps, Frankl came to the important conclusion that even in the most absurd, heinous and inhuman conditions of our reality, our HERE AND NOW is not always what is happening around us, but WHAT WE FOCUS ON, WHAT WE CHOOSE TO THINK ABOUT: *"It is possible to take away everything from man, with the exception of one: the last particle of human freedom — freedom to select his position under any given conditions, to choose his own path".*

Viktor Frankl is a unique scientist, whose theory has stood the test of time. It's hard to think of another scientist whose theory would have been such an unprecedented test of life. At the price of personal tragedy, Viktor Frankl proved that *"the greatest chance of survival, even in such extreme conditions belonged to those who saw into the future and the work that was waiting for them"* Such people are those who at the price of, maybe incredible efforts, CREATED THEIR REALITY. According to the Frankl's obser-

WHAT IS OUR REALITY?

vations, the **greatest chances of survival** did not belong to those who had good physical health, but to **those who had a strong spirit** — those who clearly saw and PERCEIVED the meaning of their life, the REASON they had to live and SURVIVE.

Thus, the conclusion we can draw from this story, is that **the reality of each person is not what is happening** but that which they CHOOSE TO FOCUS THEIR MINDS ON. As we can see, even during the Holocaust while some people went crazy from what was happening around them, others managed to survive in the midst of that horror while keeping their sanity, just because they focused on those things that they chose to think about — loved ones, themselves engaged in a favourite business or reflecting on the scriptures. While others were being shot dead, these people, instead of worrying about their own death, lived in another reality because at that time they contemplated on the Torah, the Bible — on the principles laid therein for example *"...love your enemies and do good to them that hate you..."* (The Bible, Luke 6:27). And because of this, these people were able to survive, they were able to come out, because they CREATED THEIR OWN REALITY — placed themselves in another atmosphere.

HOW TO MANAGE YOUR THOUGHTS AND FEELINGS

Only by learning to recognize and actually control your thoughts, your feelings, will you understand how to create the world you live in. This is your freedom and your strength, and when you become the conscious creator of your destiny and start using the law of attraction, you begin the life you cannot imagine.

FROM THE MOVIE 'THE SECRET'

Let's clarify what determines the feelings and behavior of every man. Understanding this mechanism will enable us make our feelings serve us — learn to manage them. By subjugating our thoughts and emotions, we can create the preferred world we want to live in. But we will talk about it in the next subchapter. Earlier on, we talked to you, dear reader, about offences and **self-pity**. Now, SELF-PITY IS INEVITABLE in the life of a person who has not learned to CONTROL THEIR MINDS. As we found out, what a man focuses on determines his reality, **because reality is not what is happening to you, it is what you decide to fix your attention on.**

For example, if someone passing by me decided to push me or step on my toes, this can be taken either literally or figuratively. I now face two choices: the first is to focus on the pain and the result will be resentment, anger or desire for revenge. This happens only if I focus on how I feel. The second response I can choose when my toes get stepped on, is to recall the words of Jesus Christ written in one of the greatest books of mankind — the Bible: "If *someone slaps you on one cheek, turn to them the other also ...*" (Luke 6:29). Even Jesus himself, when he was crucified, cried not for vengeance, but for mercy towards those who had caused Him so much pain and suffering.

If I focus on the pain and not on the truth, then I have made a wrong choice because evil can be defeated only by good — evil becomes my reality, leading to further multiplication of that evil. When the focus is on the pain, it implies that am self-centered and this is a 'fertile' ground for the development of self-pity. At that moment, am only looking at the situation from my 'feelings' point of view instead of the interests of other people. So if I shift the focus from 'ME', then I become free from the selfish need to protect myself at all costs — to prove my innocence to others or vent my anger, resentment and bitterness. I refuse to multiply the evil in this world, responding to someone in the same way as they did towards me; I thereby choose to make this world a better, kinder and brighter place — even if I have to pay with my personal inconvenience. In order to be a good example, I need to cope with my pain, which is quite real. I need to make the decision to forgive the person who has caused me so much pain and discomfort, and even find ways to do some good towards him or her.

This choice also helps me to overcome my 'animal' instincts (which we looked at in the first chapters of this book). If I live unconsciously, being driven by instincts or reflexes, then when my foot is hurt, my reflexes will cry, "Fight back!", "Revenge!" But by obeying this negative voice, I automatically reduce myself to the level of an animal. On the other hand, if I consider myself a sensible man (Homo Sapiens), who is always guided by reasoning, then I take into account the true facts of my life principles and values. In this way, I rise above my instincts that try to drive me towards the level of any thought-less animal, and I begin to win against the feeling of revenge which are ready to devour me in the heat of rage. Therefore, when my foot is trodden upon, I have the choice to either react as a sensible man or be like a foolish animal. Which choice do you usually make, dear reader?

WHAT COMES FIRST — EXISTENCE OR CONSCIOUSNESS? (HOW TO CREATE THE WORLD YOU WANT TO LIVE IN)

So, we have found out how to manage our thoughts and feelings. Now I want us to look at how we can create the world we want to live in, for therein lies our freedom and our strength, and that's when we are able to become a conscious creator of our destiny.

If you remember, at the core of the Soviet world order were the postulates of Marxism-Leninism, one of which says: *"Existence determines consciousness"*. This formulation was derived from the words of Karl Marx (1818–1883), German philosopher, sociologist, economist, writer, poet, political journalist and social activist, who in the Preface to his work, entitled 'A *Critique of Political Economy*' (1859) said, " *It is not the consciousness of men that determines their existence, but their social existence that determines their consciousness.*" That cliche was never subjected to any criticism through the long decades of Soviet power; each Soviet person firmly held on to it. It was believed that the environment, people and lifestyle shaped human consciousness, external conditions determine the inner content and the quality of the person. Therefore, reasonable efforts were made to raise the welfare of the population — to increase the level of consumption of milk, meat and eggs per capita, to issue apartments to everyone, to strive to ensure that every family was wall to wall carpeted with crystals on the wall, as it was piously believed that this will instil moral and ethical qualities in the Soviet people. They were convinced that in this case, no one will want to engage in looting, rape or genuinely want to get drunk: after all if the external conditions of life are wonderful, what else does a man need? Live and be happy! But for some reason, this did not work.

The change in the external life conditions was viewed as a panacea for all social ills. It was believed that if you created favorable conditions for a person, they would no longer be a person, but will turn into 'gold'! Conversely, it was believed that if a person leads an anti-social lifestyle — not studying, not working, committing all sorts of crimes, then this was only because of the pressures from his harsh environment. So who would be inclined to break the law if placed in the environment of honest and hardworking people? The first response of any idler or 'parasite' would automatically be to improve. But is this really so?

Probably many of you are familiar with this mentality that gets lodged in the consciousness of many for years, and for some, throughout life: *"I have no luck in life — I was born and raised in a poor family, in a poor country, among people engaged only in survival. Now, if I was born and raised among the culturally affluent people, because of the new social circle I'd have had a chance to get rich, and my children would be better off."*

Some American scientists from the USA decided to check how true that statement was. In 1994, an experiment was performed in the United States of America, termed 'Moving to Opportunity'. In that experiment, the scientists randomly chose 4,600 poor American families of those who wished to participate in the program. Then they randomly divided these families into three groups:

1. Families who were resettled in poor areas

2. Families who were resettled in the rich areas

3. Control-group families that did not move at all

Upon completion of the experiment, the National Bureau of Economic Research (NBER) published its final report with a statistical analysis of the results. What was the outcome of the experiment? Well, it turned out that good neighbors do not affect the level of unemployment among those moved, as well as the academic performance of children in these families.

Observational data covering 4–7 years showed no fall in the number of arrests for crimes related to violence among the youth of the relocated families compared with other families involved in the experiment. That is to say that moving to more affluent neighborhoods did not necessarily translate to reducing criminogenic attitudes among the people who were relocated. Moving to the area with a wealthier population almost had no impact on objective indicators of family well-being, such as income or education level.

Thus, we can conclude that only WHAT WE ACHIEVE INWARDLY, CHANGES OUR EXTERNAL REALITY. It is only those changes that we acquire as a result of our efforts in the process of working on ourselves that can change what our lives can become. No external force is able to change the person inside. Improving the housing conditions or the distribution of financial resources so that everyone always had enough money, will not make a person any more happy, morally upright, rich or successful. All the positive changes that occur in human life, first happen within. **All real and long-term transformation that is possible through man, only happens from the inside out.** So let me make the following statement: WE DEFINE (CREATE) OUR LIFE. In this regard, I wish to bring to your attention, dear reader, the following parable:

> *It was snowing. The weather was windless, and large fluffy snowflakes were slowly circling in a bizarre dance, slowly approaching the earth. Two snowflakes flying next to each other, decided to start a conversation. Fearful of losing each other, they held hands, and one of them said cheerfully,*
> - *"How nice to fly, enjoy the flight!"*
> - *"We don't fly, we just fall," sadly replied the second.*
> - *The first snowflake went on, "Soon we will meet with the earth and turn into a white fluffy blanket!"*

- *"No, we fall towards death, while on earth we just crush," argued the second*
- *"We will be streams and strive into the sea. We will live forever!" said the first.*
- *"No, we will melt and disappear forever," objected the second.*

Finally they got tired of arguing. They let go of each other and each snowflake fell to meet the fate it had chosen for itself.

This wonderful parable well illustrates how given the same conditions, it is still possible to draw opposite conclusions and come to completely different results. Indeed, each person is free to determine what lies ahead of them. It depends on one's mind — what they choose to focus on, think about or fix their attention on. **Our reality is what we focus our attention on, where we are in the HERE AND NOW.** When we develop our own reality, we create our own life. We are the creators of our own life, and nobody else will do for us what we need to do in order to live better and more consciously.

In this Chapter, you have learned WHAT OUR REALITY IS. I think this was an important Chapter — to understand how to be in the HERE AND NOW. We also reviewed with you, dear reader, what affects the feelings and behavior of a person or how to manage thoughts and feelings. In conclusion, we have looked at the question: *What comes first — existence or consciousness?* And the answer to this question helped you learn how to create the world in which you live. After this Chapter, you are expected to go through the practical exercises, through which you will be able to be IN THE HERE AND NOW as often as possible.

GOLDEN NUGGETS

1. *"Man is located where his thoughts are located. Therefore try so that your thoughts would be located where YOU WANT to be."* Rabbi Nachman of Braslav, XVIII Century

2. Our reality HERE AND NOW is not always what is happening around us, but what we focus on, what we choose to think about.

3. *"He who has a WHY to live for can bear almost any HOW."* Friedrich Nietzsche

4. The reality of each person is not what is actually happening, but what his or her mind is focused on.

5. What we achieve inwardly changes our external reality.

6. Self-pity is inevitable in the life of someone who has not learned to control his or her mind.

7. All real and long-term transformation that is possible through man, only happens from the inside out.

8. We determine and form our lives ourselves.

9. What we focus our attention on — where we stay HERE AND NOW, becomes our reality.

10. We are the creators of life, and nobody else will do for us what we need to do in order to live better and more consciously.

SELF-ASSESSMENT

1. **Are you able to control your thoughts?**
   a) Unrealistic! (0)
   b) No (1)
   c) With difficulty (2)
   d) Yes (4)

2. **Do you feel like the master of your own destiny?**
   a) No (0)
   b) Rarely (1)
   c) Very often (3)
   d) Always (4)

3. **How often are you discouraged by what is happening around you?**
   a) Quite often (0)
   b) Sometimes (1)
   c) Rarely (3)
   d) Never (4)

Self assessment results

0–3 points

Sorry! Being IN THE HERE AND NOW is currently almost impossible for you. You are hardly in control of the changes you experience as a result of what is happening. It is most likely that you are just floating through life, not taking anything that could help you begin to increasingly monitor your progress. But don't despair! Studying this book can help you to correct the situation.

4–8 points

You can control your thoughts with varying success. You find it hard to shape your reality because you cannot always and confidently choose what you want to think about at the moment. To help you become the rightful creator of your own life, we recommend that you read this book until the end. From it you will learn what can be done practically, to always be IN THE HERE AND NOW and to independently determine the further development of your life.

9–12 points

Congratulations! You can monitor the progress of your thoughts and focus your mind on what you think is necessary. Moreover, you are the creator of your life, which is quite rare in this world. You are able to help those who need this, do not hesitate to do so!

RECOMMENDATIONS
ON CARRYING OUT THE
PRACTICAL TASKS

1. ATTENTION! The practical tasks listed after each Chapter are not just for reading; you need them. With my years of experience with people, I know that oftentimes, people perform these tasks just 'to tick the box', as if in school; but this is your life, this is for you, take the assignments seriously.

2. For maximum results we recommend you perform the tasks within 24 hours, otherwise, leaving them for later, you are distancing yourself from your destiny and your success.

3. To answer all the questions, work out the practical tasks in a serene and tranquil environment. Find a quiet place where no one will be able to interfere; perhaps a time when no one is at home; or at night when everyone is asleep.

4. Be sure to reflect on the previous Chapter and go over all the items which you emphasized for yourself. Remember the decisions you made and write down your subsequent actions.

5. Certainly put specific time deadlines planned, and define restrictions which you will apply in relation to yourself; it will help you not to shelve implementation of the decisions you made.

6. Find someone to whom you could be accountable regarding your decisions, who could remind you of them — a kind of partner in working on yourself.

PRACTICAL TASKS

1. What determines our reality? Analyze your own present reality.

2. What determines the feelings and behavior of a person? What principles have you learned from this Chapter — How to manage your thoughts and feelings?

3. So what comes first — EXISTENCE or CONSCIOUSNESS? What principles governing the creation of your world have you personally learned from this Chapter and hope to use in the future for guidance?

PRACTICAL EXERCISES

*If you have decided to learn to focus on one
thing, do not rely on the contribution from
the external environment to do it, create a
workspace the way you like it most.*

ADAM JACKSON

So, throughout the book, we looked at HOW TO BE
IN THE HERE AND NOW or how to stop soaring in the
clouds. It is now time to learn how to apply your knowledge
practically. These practical exercises will help you increase
your level of alertness, concentration and focus, improve
your ability to concentrate — that is, they will help to improve your skills to be IN THE HERE AND NOW, and will
also help to get rid of anxiety and unrest.

1. Watching your breath

We all breathe, but often we do not notice it much. It is
scientifically proven that the mental apparatus and breath
are connected. Rhythmic breathing helps you focus your
mind on the right thing. To develop your ability to be IN
THE HERE AND NOW, start to follow the breath, not
slowing down and not controlling it: a minimum of 10
minutes every day for one month. Ideally 5 times a day for
10 minutes, for 21 days.

Such breathing exercises help to raise the level of your
concentration as well as get rid of the 'garbage' in your

mind, obsessions and sinful thoughts. As a wise man once said, "Don't forget to empty the trash... from the bucket... out from your head... from your life!"

2. Do not think about more than one thing

Most people jump from one thing to another. To be the HERE AND NOW, we must set ourselves the task of thinking about not more than one thing at the same time. "Don't you start a new business, until you complete the previous one," said Max Frei, "Everything started should be done to the end, even if we are talking about mere trifles."

I can illustrate this principle using my own life — I have personal effectiveness in all aspects of life. With all the many things that I have to do, I am able to clearly distinguish between them. For example — when am eating, then at that moment, I just focussing only on the eating, and at that time it is better not to approach me with other questions because you will not get sensible answers!

3. Make a decision not to worry about anything

In order to effectively be IN THE HERE AND NOW every second of your life, it is extremely important to learn to put aside that which is troubling you. Remember WORRIES DO NOT BRING SOLUTIONS INTO THE PREVAILING SITUATION! Because of this, it is important to adopt the following principle: *I only deal with solutions (to problems), but not indulge in worries. If something is troubling me, I find ways to convert this concern into concrete actions to help eliminate the cause of such emotions.*

As soon as worry sets in, it is necessary to work with the following rules-set:

1. If the situation can be changed, then begin to seek a way out of the problem.

2. If there is no way for you to influence the situation, then you should just stop thinking about it.

Imagine this situation: Your child is on a school bus which is involved in an accident. The first reaction, which is quite natural is — thumping panic. But HYSTERIA is the REACTION of people who have not learned to GOVERN THEMSELVES. The most reasonable reaction that can be taken in this situation is to convert the whole experience of the children on board into concrete actions for example:

- What specifically can help them at this very moment?
- What should I do?
- Where are they now?
- What is the address of the place?
- Who do we need to call?
- Who needs to resolve this situation?

Here is another example: Having a headache. What most of us do in such a situation is to go about telling everyone how terrible the headache is; the first time — in the morning, then in the afternoon and even in the evening! We should rather find out what could be the cause of the headache and then use the remedies to eliminate the pain. But if one is overwhelmed with the need for pity, then of course, they will start by telling everyone about their headache.

4. Spell and pronounce words backwards

You can use your first name and surname as training phrases (easy for those with short names). Moreover, you need to pronounce the resulting words formed by the letters, not just spell them. For example using the names: **John McDonald**, in reverse order would be: **dlanoDcM nhoJ**. This helps to develop your concentration.

5. You must recall the 10 sounds that you hear while in the room

Another version of this same exercise is to close your eyes and try to describe what the people around you are wearing.

The more you practice these exercises, the better you will become at being HERE AND NOW. The second version of the exercise will enable you to notice not only people's bodies but the people themselves — their faces, names. Our problem is that we often do not notice each other. We can just get past somebody without paying any attention to him or her. And the reason we don't remember people is because of poor concentration. This is still an indication of how attentive or absent minded we are to each other.

6. The development of a sense of urgency

The **current** is what is important HERE AND NOW, it is always in the present tense. The **current** is:

- Essential, a burning issue
- Topical, vital
- Important on the agenda for the moment

The **current** changes all the time. In a healthy person, the feeling of relevance is steady and constant but his assessment changes all the time just like the view from a carriage window. By relevance we mean your personal relevance — your own experience. You cannot go through what is relevant to another person.

The purpose of this practice is to come to the feeling that you are in a continuous flow process. This exercise will allow you to increase your awareness of what you do and how you do it.

Here is an exercise to help you: Try, within five minutes, to make up sentences, expressing the fact that you are conscious of the moment. You could start each sentence with the following: *"Now ...", "In this moment ...", "Here and now ..."*

For example: *"Now* I am in my body, sitting here on a soft chair, the chair is in a room, the room is in the house ...", *"This is the ... day of the week, in the month of ..., in the year 20....., in the twenty-first century. Here and now, am doing so-and-so."* Come up with about 10 variants of such sentences to address the following:

- What are you doing?
- Do you realise where you are?
- Are you aware of what is going on?

In conclusion, I want to say that learning to be IN THE HERE AND NOW is extremely important for all of us. In order to reach greater heights in life, you must continue putting more effort into this.

CONCLUSION

Here comes the end of our journey dear reader. Please do understand that each person came to this planet to learn certain things, and because we are all different, the lessons for each of us are different too. The most important thing that you should remember is that **we are here to learn the right lessons and not to change other people.** WE CAME TO THIS PLANET TO CHANGE OURSELVES! No one else can learn for you a lesson that you ought to learn, or do what you should do, because in that case you learn nothing. Even if someone else like your mum, dad or some other good family member were to make you do it against your will, you would remain in the same state — nothing will ever change in your life. If you do not involve yourself in the process of change, if you don't want to learn, if you don't crave for positive change in your own life, then don't be surprised if you re-create the same problems that you have repeatedly suffered in the past. As the Russian saying goes, *"They keep treading on the same rake"* — you will again and again be earning the same painful blows.

Did you know that some people don't want to be freed from their illnesses? Of course these people will claim that they do not want to hurt but this is contrary to their actions. Statistics indicates that only 30% of people who go to the doctors follow their doctor's instructions. Many of those who go to the doctor, don't do it to be healthy, but only to alleviate symptoms and the pain. They are not really trying to understand and eradicate the problem that caused the sickness. It often seems that there is an unwritten agreement between the doctor and the patient — the doctor promises not to treat the patient if they just pretend to follow the advice given. The doctor is getting paid for this while the patient has another excuse to justify their disease.

In life there is a lot of good out there and any effort we make to picking from this can practically help us change our lives — get rid of destructive habits (like not being HERE AND NOW) and acquire useful life skills that can help us improve the quality of our lives. It is very important to BE READY TO WORK ON YOURSELF, TO MAINTAIN A THIRST FOR PERSONAL TRANSFORMATION AND A WILLINGNESS TO LEARN FROM ANYONE WHO IS MORE SUCCESSFUL IN A SPECIFIC AREA AT THE MOMENT. Because when someone imposes something on us, forcing, coercing, attempting to push and engage in moralizing us, experience shows that such a disservice is a little confusing. We can do the person the favor and then drop everything once they are out of sight even though it is for our own benefit. Or we can pretend that we are interested in the advice, yet never do anything about it nor put in the minimal effort, just because we have full confidence that "this, as usual, will not help".

In the beginning of the book, I mentioned about people who, after having lived their lives, discovered that 'life has passed like a dream'. We wondered what to do to ensure our lives do not become a sleep in reality, only to 'awake' from such ruinous slumber, when our entire life, in essence, has

lost its meaning and even the 'bright colors' of our existence. Probably, Seneca (4 BC — 65 AD), a Roman stoic philosopher, poet, statesman, educator of Nero and one of the
largest representatives of stoicism, too, had wondered about
that, when he wrote: *"Every day should be lived as if it were
our last"*, otherwise it would be vanity to spend our allotted
precious time sleep-waking, not being HERE AND NOW.

SUNDAY ADELAJA'S BIOGRAPHY

Pastor Sunday Adelaja is the Founder and Senior Pastor of The Embassy of the Blessed Kingdom of God for All Nations Church in Kyiv, Ukraine.

Sunday Adelaja is a Nigerian-born Leader, Thinker, Philosopher, Transformation Strategist, Pastor, Author and Innovator who lives in Kiev, Ukraine.

At 19, he won a scholarship to study in the former Soviet Union. He completed his master's program in Belorussia State University with distinction in journalism.

At 33, he had built the largest evangelical church in Europe — The Embassy of the Blessed Kingdom of God for All Nations.

Sunday Adelaja is one of the few individuals in our world who has been privileged to speak in the United Nations, Israeli Parliament, Japanese Parliament and the United States Senate.

The movement he pioneered has been instrumental in reshaping lives of people in the Ukraine, Russia and about 50 other nations where he has his branches.

His congregation, which consists of ninety-nine percent white Europeans, is a cross-cultural model of the church for the 21st century.

His life mission is to advance the Kingdom of God on earth by raising a generation of history mak-

ers who will live for a cause larger, bigger and greater than themselves. Those who will live like Jesus and transform every sphere of the society in every nation as a model of the Kingdom of God on earth.

His economic empowerment program has succeeded in raising over 200 millionaires in the short period of three years.

Sunday Adelaja is the author of over 300 books, many of which are translated into several languages including Russian, English, French, Chinese, German, etc.

His work has been widely reported by world media outlets such as The Washington Post, The Wall Street Journal, New York Times, Forbes, Associated Press, Reuters, CNN, BBC, German, Dutch and French national television stations.

Pastor Sunday is happily married to his "Princess" Bose Dere-Adelaja. They are blessed with three children: Perez, Zoe and Pearl.

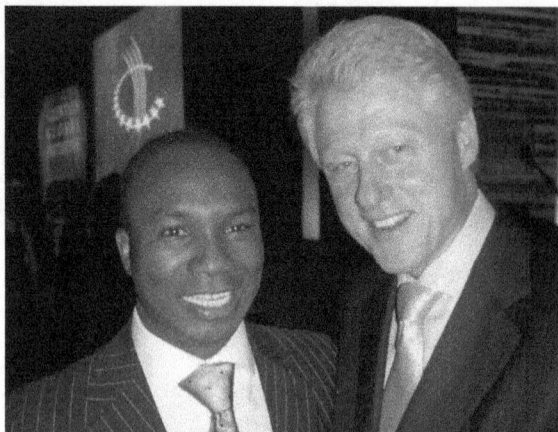

Bill Clinton —
42Nd President Of The
United States (1993–2001),
Former Arcansas State
Governor

Ariel "Arik" Sharon —
Israeli Politician, Israeli
Prime Minister (2001–2006)

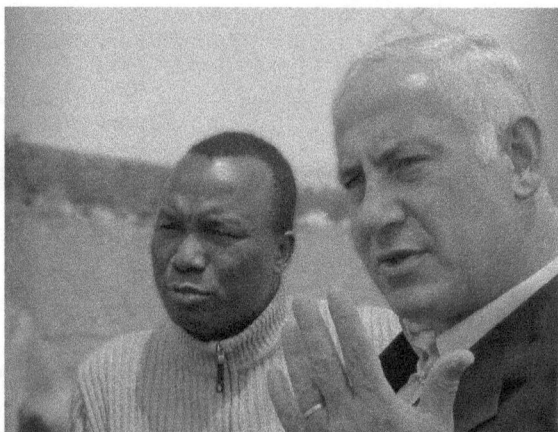

Benjamin Netanyahu —
Statesman Of Israel. Israeli
Prime Minister (1996–1999),
Acting Prime Minister
(From 2009)

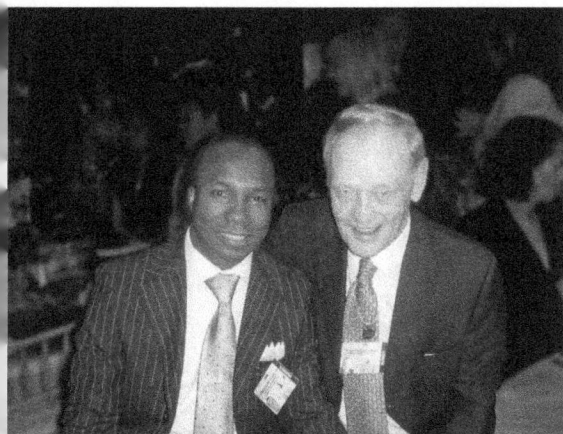

Jean ChrEtien —
Canadian Politician,
20Th Prime Minister Of
Canada, Minister Of Justice
Of Canada, Head Of Liberan
Party Of Canada

Rudolph Giuliani —
American Political Actor,
Mayor Of New York Served
From 1994 To 2001. Actor
Of Republican Party

Colin Powell —
Is An American Statesman
And A Retired Four-Star
General In The Us Army,
65Th United States Secretary
Of State

Peter J. Daniels —
Is A Well-Known And
Respected Australian
Christian International
Business Statesman Of
Substance

Madeleine
Korbel Albright —
An American Politician And
Diplomat, 64[Th] United States
Secretary Of State

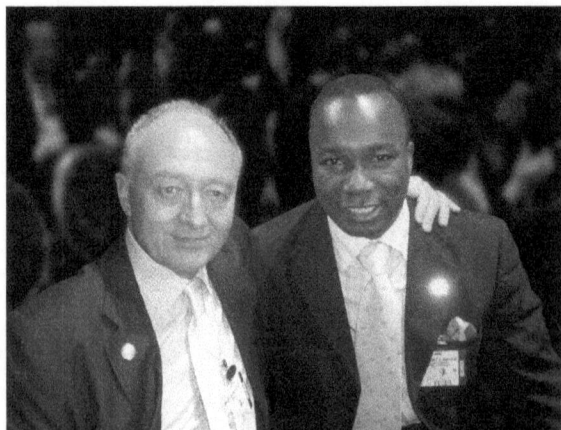

Kenneth Robert
Livingstone —
An English Politician,
1[St] Mayor Of London
(4 May 2000 – 4 May
2008), Labour Party
Representative

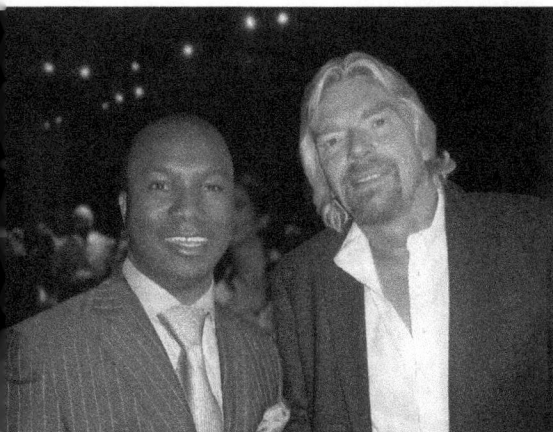

Sir Richard Charles Nicholas Branson —
English Business Magnate, Investor And Philanthropist. He Founded The *Virgin Group,* Which Controls More Than 400 Companies

Mel Gibson —
American Actor And Filmmaker

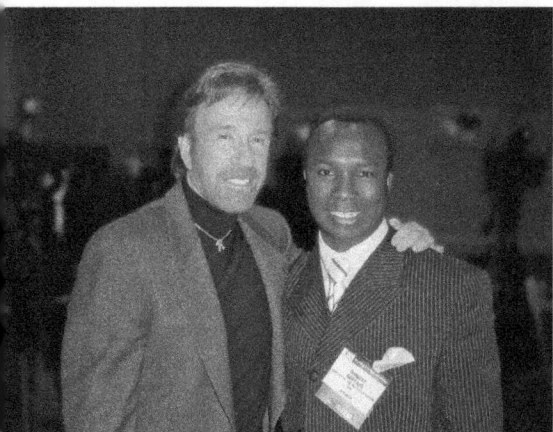

Chuck Norris —
American Martial Artist, Actor, Film Producer And Screenwriter

Christopher Tucker —
American Actor
And Comedian

Bernice Albertine King —
American Minister Best
Known As The Youngest
Child Of Civil Rights Leaders
Martin Luther King Jr. And
Coretta Scott King Andrew

Andrew Young — American
Politician, Diplomat, And
Activist, 14Th United States
Ambassador To The United
Nations, 55Th Mayor Of
Atlanta

General Wesley Kanne Clark — 4-Star General And Nato Supreme Allied Commander

Dr. Sunday Adelaja's family: Perez, Pearl, Zoe and Pastor Bose Adelaja

FOLLOW
SUNDAY ADELAJA
ON SOCIAL MEDIA

Subscribe And Read Pastor Sunday's Blog:
www.sundayadelajablog.com
Follow these links and listen to over 200
of Pastor Sunday's Messages free of charge:
http://sundayadelajablog.com/content/
Follow Pastor Sunday on Twitter:
www.twitter.com/official_pastor

Join Pastor Sunday's Facebook page to stay in touch:
www.facebook.com/pastor.
sunday.adelaja
Visit our websites for more
information about Pastor
Sunday's ministry:
http://www.godembassy.com
http://www.pastorsunday.com
http://sundayadelaja.de

CONTACT

FOR DISTRIBUTION OR TO ORDER
BULK COPIES OF THIS BOOK,
PLEASE CONTACT US:

USA
CORNERSTONE PUBLISHING
info@thecornerstonepublishers.com
+1 (516) 547-4999
www.thecornerstonepublishers.com

AFRICA
SUNDAY ADELAJA MEDIA LTD.
E-mail: btawolana@hotmail.com
+2348187518530, +2348097721451, +2348034093699

LONDON, UK
PASTOR ABRAHAM GREAT
abrahamagreat@gmail.com
+447711399828, +441908538141

KIEV, UKRAINE
pa@godembassy.org
Mobile: +380674401958

BEST SELLING BOOKS BY DR. SUNDAY ADELAJA
AVAILABLE ON AMAZON.COM AND OKADABOOKS.COM

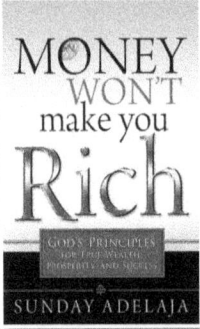

MONEY WON'T make you Rich — GOD'S PRINCIPLES FOR TRUE WEALTH, PROSPERITY AND SOCIETY — SUNDAY ADELAJA

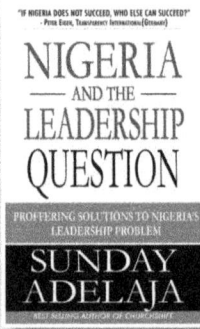

"IF NIGERIA DOES NOT SUCCEED, WHO ELSE CAN SUCCEED?" — PETER EIGEN, TRANSPARENCY INTERNATIONAL (GERMANY)

NIGERIA — AND THE — LEADERSHIP QUESTION — PROFFERING SOLUTIONS TO NIGERIA'S LEADERSHIP PROBLEM — SUNDAY ADELAJA — BEST SELLING AUTHOR OF CHURCHSHIFT

MYLES MUNROE — ... FINDING ANSWERS TO WHY GOOD PEOPLE DIE TRAGIC AND EARLY DEATHS — SUNDAY ADELAJA

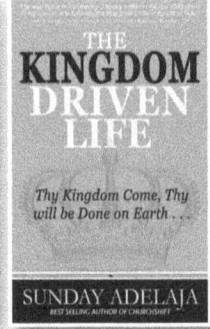

THE KINGDOM DRIVEN LIFE — Thy Kingdom Come, Thy will be Done on Earth . . . — SUNDAY ADELAJA — BEST SELLING AUTHOR OF CHURCHSHIFT

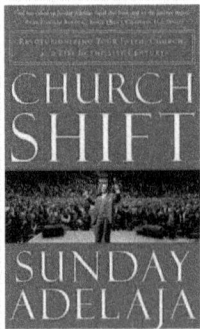

CHURCH SHIFT — SUNDAY ADELAJA

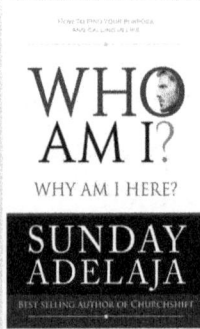

WHO AM I? — WHY AM I HERE? — SUNDAY ADELAJA — BEST SELLING AUTHOR OF CHURCHSHIFT

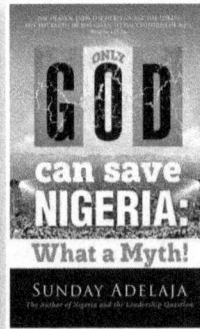

ONLY GOD can save NIGERIA: What a Myth! — SUNDAY ADELAJA — The Author of Nigeria and the Leadership Question

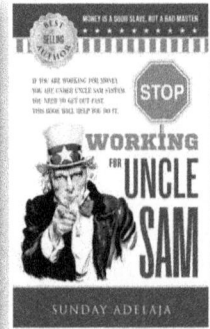

MONEY IS A GOOD SLAVE, BUT A BAD MASTER — STOP WORKING FOR UNCLE SAM — SUNDAY ADELAJA

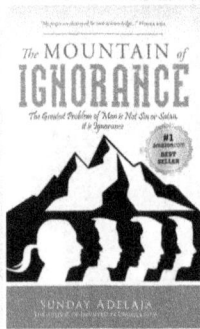

The MOUNTAIN of IGNORANCE — The Greatest Problem of Man is Not Sin or Satan, it's Ignorance — #1 BEST SELLER — SUNDAY ADELAJA

OLORUNWA — SUNDAY ADELAJA

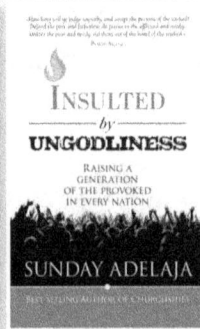

INSULTED — by — UNGODLINESS — RAISING A GENERATION OF THE PROVOKED IN EVERY NATION — SUNDAY ADELAJA — BEST SELLING AUTHOR OF CHURCHSHIFT

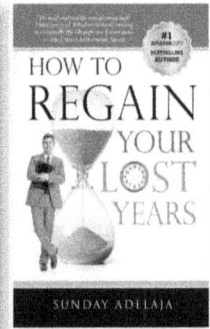

HOW TO REGAIN YOUR LOST YEARS — #1 BEST SELLING AUTHOR — SUNDAY ADELAJA

BEST SELLING BOOKS BY DR. SUNDAY ADELAJA
AVAILABLE ON AMAZON.COM AND OKADABOOKS.COM

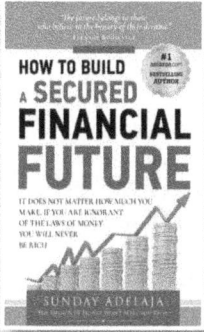

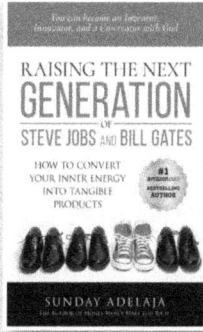

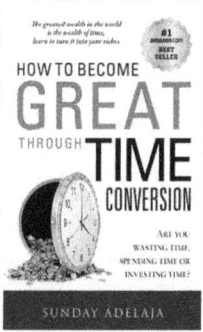

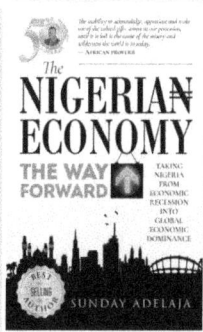

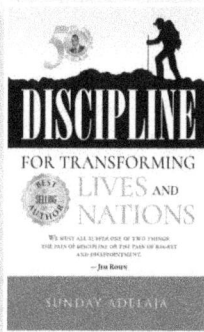

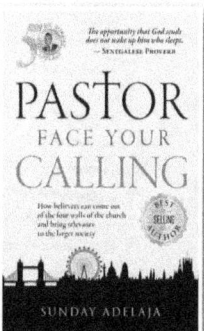

HOW TO BUILD A SECURED FINANCIAL FUTURE
IT DOES NOT MATTER HOW MUCH YOU MAKE, IF YOU ARE IGNORANT OF THE LAWS OF MONEY YOU WILL NEVER BE RICH
SUNDAY ADELAJA

CREATE YOUR OWN NET WORTH
YOUR MONEY IS TEMPORARY, YOUR NET WORTH IS ETERNAL
SUNDAY ADELAJA

RAISING THE NEXT GENERATION OF STEVE JOBS AND BILL GATES
HOW TO CONVERT YOUR INNER ENERGY INTO TANGIBLE PRODUCTS
SUNDAY ADELAJA

POVERTY MINDSET VS ABUNDANCE MINDSET
REAL POVERTY IS NOT IN THE SIZE OF YOUR POCKET BUT IN THE SIZE OF YOUR MIND

WHY YOU MUST URGENTLY BECOME A WORKAHOLIC
Work like a slave today and live like a king tomorrow
SUNDAY ADELAJA

HOW TO BECOME GREAT THROUGH TIME CONVERSION
ARE YOU WASTING TIME, SPENDING TIME OR INVESTING TIME?
SUNDAY ADELAJA

The NIGERIAN ECONOMY THE WAY FORWARD
TAKING NIGERIA FROM ECONOMIC RECESSION INTO GLOBAL ECONOMIC DOMINANCE
SUNDAY ADELAJA

DISCIPLINE FOR TRANSFORMING LIVES AND NATIONS
SUNDAY ADELAJA

PASTOR FACE YOUR CALLING
How believers can come out of the four walls of the church and bring relevance to the larger society
SUNDAY ADELAJA

WHERE THERE IS PROBLEM THERE IS MONEY
LEARN HOW OTHER'S PROBLEMS INTO YOUR STEPPING STONE TO WEALTH
SUNDAY ADELAJA

LIFE IS AN OPPORTUNITY
SUNDAY ADELAJA

The CREATIVE and INNOVATIVE POWER of a GENIUS
SUNDAY ADELAJA

GOLDEN JUBILEE SERIES BOOKS
BY DR. SUNDAY ADELAJA

FOR DISTRIBUTION OR TO ORDER BULK COPIES OF THIS BOOKS,
PLEASE CONTACT US:
USA | CORNERSTONE PUBLISHING
   E-mail: info@thecornerstonepublishers.com, +1 (516) 547-4999
   www.thecornerstonepublishers.com
AFRICA | SUNDAY ADELAJA MEDIA LTD.
   E-mail: btawolana@hotmail.com
   +2348187518530, +2348097721451, +2348034093699
LONDON, UK | PASTOR ABRAHAM GREAT
   E-mail: abrahamagreat@gmail.com, +447711399828, +441908538141
KIEV, UKRAINE |
   E-mail: pa@godembassy.org, Mobile: +380674401958

www.ingramcontent.com/pod-product-compliance
Lightning Source LLC
Chambersburg PA
CBHW022129080426
42734CB00006B/287